BEYOND THE SOLAR SYSTEM

Exploring Galaxies, Black Holes, Alien Planets, and More

A History with 21 Activities

Mary Kay Carson

CHICAGO REVIEW PRESS

Copyright © 2013 by Mary Kay Carson
All rights reserved
Published by Chicago Review Press, Incorporated
814 North Franklin Street
Chicago, Illinois 60610

ISBN 978-1-61374-544-1

Library of Congress Cataloging-in-Publication Data
Carson, Mary Kay.
Beyond the solar system : exploring galaxies, black holes, alien planets,
and more : a history with 21 activities / Mary Kay Carson.
    p. cm.
Audience: 4-6.
Includes bibliographical references and index.
ISBN 978-1-61374-544-1 (trade paper)
1. Astronomy—History—Juvenile literature. I. Title.
QB15.C37 2013
520.9—dc23
                        2012046330

Cover design: Sarah Olson
Front cover photos: Top left, artist's rendering of exoplanet UCF-1.01,
   NASA/JPL-Caltech; James Webb Space Telescope mirrors, NASA/
   MSFC/David Higginbotham; Chandra X-ray Observatory, Wizard
   Nebula, Hubble Space Telescope, artist's rendering of Cygnus X-1, all
   courtesy of NASA/CXC/M. Weiss; Very Large Array courtesy of Tom
   Uhlman Photography.
Back cover photos: Edwin Hubble, courtesy of Carnegie Observatories;
   particle accelerator, © CERN, photo by M. Brice; artist's rendering
   of exoplanet HD 189733b courtesy of ESA - C. Carreau; planet
   illustrations courtesy of NASA/CXC/M. Weiss.
Interior design: Sarah Olson

Printed in the United States of America
5 4 3 2 1

Contents

Time Line

Prehistory Humans believe that a deity or deities created their flat world covered with a dome-like sky. They mark the passage of time with lunar phases and observe visible planets with the naked eye

Ancient Times Chinese, Babylonians, Greeks, and Egyptians record their observations of the night sky

140 BC Hipparchus creates an accurate map of the 1,000 or so brightest stars

AD 100 Ptolemy publishes *The Almagest*

140 Ptolemy states that Earth is the center of the cosmos

964 Abd al-Rahman al-Sufi publishes his *Book of Fixed Stars*

1543 Nicolaus Copernicus states that the Sun is the center of the solar system

1572 After observing an exploding star, Tycho Brahe writes that changes occur in the heavens

1608 Hans Lippershey invents the refracting telescope

1609 **Galileo Galilei** builds the first astronomical telescope and begins observations

1610 Galileo Galilei observes the phases of Venus, confirming a sun-centered cosmos

1668 **Isaac Newton** builds the first reflecting telescope

1687 Isaac Newton publishes his theory of universal gravitation

1705 Edmond Halley correctly predicts the return of a comet, which reappears 53 years later

1781 William Herschel discovers Uranus, doubling the size of the solar system

1790 William Herschel discovers planetary nebulas

1860 William Huggins begins the spectral analysis of stars

1905 **Albert Einstein** publishes his theory of special relativity

1912 Henrietta Leavitt discovers a method of measuring distances of galaxies using Cepheids

1913 Ejnar Hertzsprung and Henry Russell discover the relationship between stars' color and brightness

1915   Albert Einstein publishes his theory of general relativity

1919   Sir Arthur Eddington confirms Einstein's theory of general relativity by photographing a solar eclipse

1923   Edwin Hubble proves that there are other galaxies outside the Milky Way

1926   Robert Goddard launches the first liquid-fueled rocket, paving the way for space exploration

1927   Robert Atkinson and Fritz Houtermans determine that stars are fueled by nuclear fusion

1929   **Edwin Hubble** discovers that the universe is expanding

1931   Georges Lemaître suggests the universe began in a huge explosion, the Big Bang

1932   Karl Jansky discovers cosmic radiowaves

1933   Fritz Zwicky discovers evidence of dark matter

1957   World's first satellite, *Sputnik 1*, orbits Earth

1963   Maarten Schmidt discovers quasars

1965   Arno Penzias and Robert Wilson discover cosmic microwave background from the Big Bang

1967   Jocelyn Bell discovers pulsars

1969   Donald Lynden-Bell discovers that there are supermassive black holes in the center of every galaxy

1986   **Margaret Geller** and John Huchra discover the structure in the universe

1990   *Hubble* Space Telescope launches

1991   *Compton* Gamma-Ray Observatory launches

1995   Michel Mayor and Didier Queloz discover the first exoplanet, 51 Pegasi B

1998   Teams of scientists determine that the universe's expansion is accelerating, possibly due to dark energy

1999   *Chandra* X-ray Observatory launches

2003   *Spitzer* Space Telescope launches

2009   Planet-finding space telescope *Kepler* launches

Introduction
How Do We Know About the Stars?

The next time you look up at the 3,000 or so stars visible in the night sky, put yourself in the place of a prehistoric person. Looking up at all those little lights in the darkness, imagine what you think they are. Tiny, faraway campfires that never burn out? Flying creatures carrying torches? What does what you think about the stars say about you—your beliefs, how the world works, and what controls it?

Today we know what stars are. But the journey of human understanding of what's out in space, where it all came from, and how far from us it all is has taken many centuries. Who made all these discoveries? What were these discoverers like and why did they care so much? What inventions, new tools, and technology helped them? How did we learn what we know about the universe? How are we finding out more today—and what is still unknown? These questions are what this book is about.

The Carina Nebula as captured by the *Hubble* Space Telescope. *NASA*

1 Prehistory–1600: Stargazers to Scientists

People have been exploring the **universe** for thousands of years. Even cavemen gazing up at the **stars** were investigating what lay beyond—in their own way. Early humans believed they lived on a flat world. Each day, a godlike sun crossed the sky overhead. The night sky was filled with traveling lights and a changing moon. Ancient people were wrong about Earth's pancake shape, and they didn't have a clue about **black holes**. But this didn't keep them from putting what they did know about the universe to very good use.

The Sun, moon, and stars appear to move, disappear, and reappear in the sky in predictable patterns. Figuring out, tracking, and predicting these heavenly patterns made the first clocks, calendars, and navigation tools possible. The waning and waxing moon, as it changes from full to new to full again, marks the passage of 30 sunsets and sunrises—a lunar month. The stars, Sun, moon, and the **planets** rise and set not because *they* are moving, but because *Earth* is. Our mobile planet gives us a constantly changing view of what surrounds us out in space.

Earth's tilted posture as it travels around the Sun each year creates seasons by altering day lengths and the arc of the Sun's daily path across the sky. These changes announce the coming and going of seasons. Since prehistory, the changing seasons helped people know when it was time to plant or harvest, move to winter hunting grounds, or return to summer villages.

Stars, too, are seasonal calendars. Maybe you've noticed this yourself. The pattern of stars we call the Big Dipper changes position throughout the year. Its handle points up in summer and down in winter. Its cuplike end holds water in autumn and empties it in spring.

BIG BEARS, HUNTING GODS

The Big Dipper is part of a **constellation** called Ursa Major, or the Great Bear. Constellations are groups of nearby stars that people have named after the shapes they make. They are ancient star patterns and so have the names of ancient things—mythical characters and creatures, harps, dragons, unicorns, parts of sailing ships, and now-forgotten tools.

This photograph of the Big Dipper was taken in March, when it is upside down and its handle is to the right. Can you see it? *NASA*

The Great Bear constellation, Ursa Major.
Library of Congress

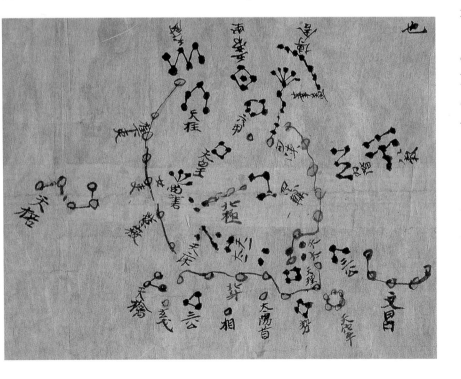

This ancient Chinese star map is part of the oldest complete star atlas known. It dates to the years 649 to 684. Look for the Big Dipper along the bottom of the chart.
British Library

Ursa Major is one of the most ancient of constellations. Humans have recognized and named it for millennia. How do we know that? People in North America as well as Eurasia call the constellation the Great Bear—even though bears haven't lived in the Middle East and Mediterranean since the end of the last ice age! The Great Bear in the sky must have been recognized by northern peoples on both sides of the waterway that was once a frozen land bridge between Siberia and Alaska 15,000 years ago.

Ursa Major was, and is, an important constellation to know if you live in the Northern Hemisphere. Its Big Dipper points out the North Star and can help you find your way. Sailors and travelers can use the stars to navigate their way across oceans and deserts without landmarks.

Constellations also have calendar duties. Virgo, the Maiden, appears in the spring with an armful of grain, telling farmers it's time to sow crops—and watch out for floods. Orion, the Mighty Hunter, is a constellation that heralds winter. In the southern hemisphere, Orion announces summer and looks different since it's flipped over. The Yolngu aboriginal people of Australia call the star grouping Julpan, a canoe filled with brothers who have a fish on the line.

GREEKS, THE ORIGINAL SCIENCE GEEKS

By 1500 BC the Sumerians, Babylonians, Indians, Chinese, and Egyptians all had skilled observers of the heavens. These "star namers" (the meaning of the word **astronomer**) had important duties in ancient civilizations. But it was the ancient Greeks who put the science in what's celestial. They turned star naming into the science of **astronomy**.

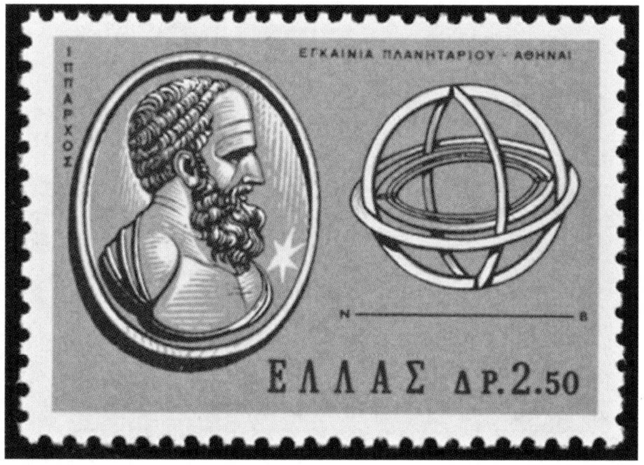

Greece issued this stamp picturing Hipparchus and an astrolabe to commemorate the opening of the Eugenides Planetarium in Athens in 1965.

Find Polaris

activity

Because our planet moves around the Sun, our view of the backdrop of constellations constantly changes. Autumn night skies feature different stars than springtime ones. But ***Polaris,*** *the North Star, doesn't move across the sky from season to season; it always remains above us and always points to the north. This is why Polaris has been used in navigation for millennia. Here's how you can spot the North Star for yourself.*

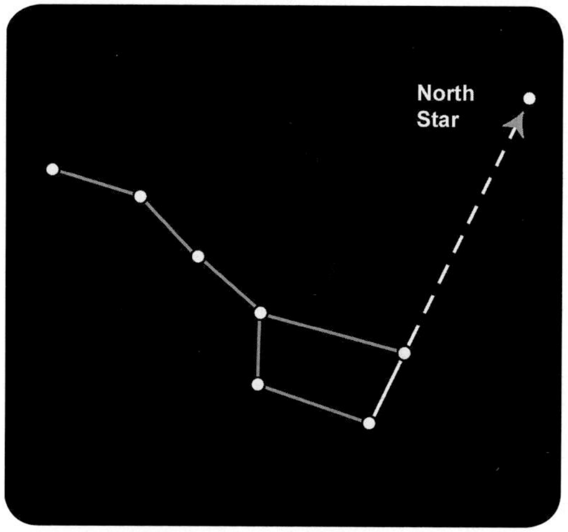

YOU'LL NEED

- Clear night sky

1. Find the Big Dipper. It's a star grouping in Ursa Major, a constellation in the northern hemisphere. Seven bright stars make up the Big Dipper in the northern or northwest sky. They form the shape of a dipper, or ladle, with a curved handle. Note: The Big Dipper's cuplike end is upright in autumn and overturned in spring, and its handle is pointed up in summer and down in winter.
2. Look at the cup end of the Big Dipper. The side of the cup farther from the handle is its "pouring edge." The two stars that make up this pouring edge of the Big Dipper will point you toward Polaris.
3. Imagine a line that connects the bottom pouring-edge star to the top one and then continues onward. The star that this imaginary line points to is Polaris, the North Star.

Hipparchus was born around 190 BC. He was a weather watcher as a young man, making records of rainfall and winds. For much of his life, Hipparchus spent his time on the Greek isle of Rhodes, observing the stars. He recorded the position, size, and brightness of many hundreds of stars. Another ancient Greek astronomer updated Hipparchus's work. Ptolemy (c.100 AD–c.170) wrote the first astronomy textbook, called *The Almagest*. It had a catalog of all the known stars—more than 1,000. The book also explained why Earth is at the center of the universe.

An Earth-centered, or **geocentric**, view of the universe was already accepted among ancient Greek philosophers. The Greeks saw the universe as a series of nested shells.

Ancient Greek astronomer Ptolemy.

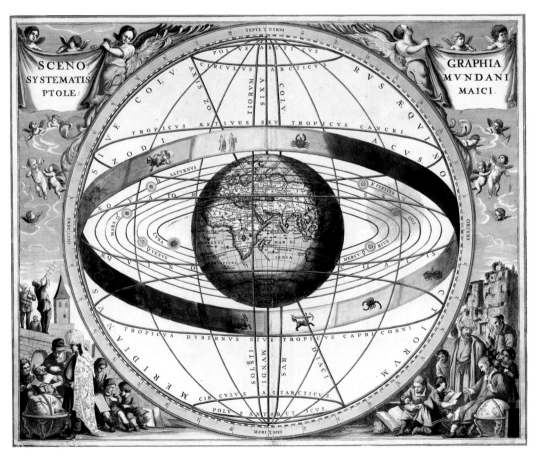

This 1660 chart shows Ptolemy's universe with the Earth at its center.

The stars were located in the outermost shell, rising and setting in the night sky as it turned around the Earth. The Sun, moon, and five known planets—Mercury, Venus, Mars, Jupiter, and Saturn—also orbited our motionless world. What Ptolemy added was an explanation that cleared up the theory's trouble spots. Until Ptolemy, no one could explain some of the movements of the five visible planets.

The word *planet* means "wanderer" because these lights in the night sky wander across the background of stars in odd ways—speeding up, moving backward, changing brightness, etc. The **Ptolemaic system** explained these oddities with mini-orbits within **orbits**, called **epicycles**. Mars, for instance, didn't just loop around Earth. It also moved in circles (its epicycle), bringing it a bit closer and farther from Earth as it looped around—sort of like a carousel ride on which you sit in a spinning car as the whole thing goes around. Ptolemy sealed the deal on his theory with some impressive and convincing geometry.

Few had trouble with the unmoving Earth aspect of Ptolemy's system. Humans don't feel Earth spinning or hurtling through space around the Sun. "Those who think it paradoxical that the Earth, having such a great **weight**, is not supported by anything and yet does not move, seem to me to be making the mistake of judging on the basis of their own experience instead of taking into account the peculiar nature of the universe," wrote Ptolemy.

Ptolemy tapped into the belief systems of the time. No one expected the heavens to play by the same rules as Earth. After all, the heavens were the domain of gods, goddesses, and forces that controlled lives and fates. Even though it was awkwardly complicated, the Ptolemaic system was popular for 15 centuries, or 1,500 years.

ALLAH'S PATH OF UNDERSTANDING

Ptolemy's ideas went far beyond Greece. He worked in the Egyptian city of Alexandria. Islamic and European astronomers through

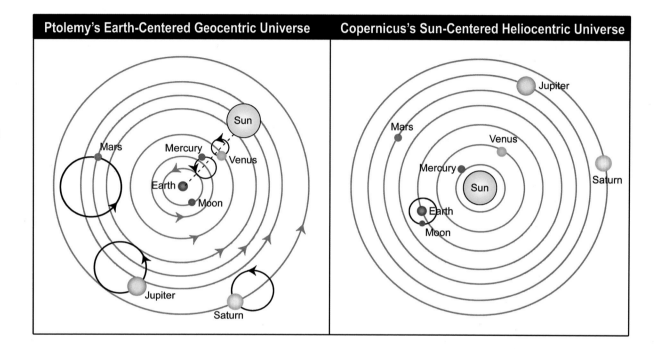

Ptolemy's Earth-Centered Geocentric Universe

Copernicus's Sun-Centered Heliocentric Universe

Ptolemy on a Plate

activity

Ptolemy's invention of epicycles made his Earth-centered system seem to work. Epicycles are the mini-orbits that the "planets" (not Earth) make around an invisible point as they circle Earth in orbits called **deferents***.*

This system of epicycles within deferents is complicated. But it seemed right because it matched the observable movements of the planets in the night sky. The theory wrongly accounted for why Mars moves backward in **retrograde***, or why Jupiter moves slower or faster depending on the time of year.*

In this activity, you'll see for yourself how Ptolemy's grand illusion matched these variations in the night sky.

YOU'LL NEED

➡ Poster board, index card, or heavy paper

➡ Ruler

➡ Scissors

➡ Markers or colored pencils

➡ Small balls (optional)

➡ Glue (optional)

➡ 2 paper plates, one large and one small, or one large and one small circle of cardboard

➡ 2 brads (paper fasteners)

➡ Liquid correction fluid (optional)

1. Cut out a small circle from an index card or heavy paper about 2 inches (5 cm) in diameter. This circle represents an epicycle. Draw a red circle on its edge to represent Mars. If you're using the small balls, glue a small red ball near the edge of the circle. Label it **Mars**.

2. If your two plates are the same size, cut one down to make it slightly smaller than the other plate. Set the 2-inch-wide circle (5 cm) near the edge of the smaller plate. Push a brad through both plates and fold it back to attach them. Make

sure it turns freely. This spinning circle is the epicycle on the edge of the deferent. (You can use liquid correction fluid to blot out the epicycle's fastener. It's an invisible point.)

3. The small plate is the deferent, Mars's orbit around Earth. Turn the large plate over, center the smaller plate on top of it, and push a brad through to attach them. Make sure it turns freely. The paper fastener in the center is Earth. Draw a little blue circle around it or glue down a blue ball. Label it **Earth**.

4. Put Ptolemy's universe into motion! Turn the larger deferent circle while simultaneously turning the epicycle. Think about being on Earth and how Mars would move in the night sky over time. Use a ruler or pencil to create a line of sight between Earth and Mars at different positions of the deferent's and epicycle's orbits.

Paper plates

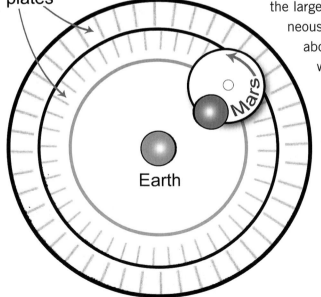

Earth

This 18th century astrolabe is from Persia. The hook-shaped pointers on the top indicate the positions of the brightest stars. *Andrew Dunn*

Abd al-Rahman al-Sufi (AD 903–986)

Isfahan, Persia, where al-Sufi lived his life, is today part of Iran. The Persian astronomer was known in Europe as Azophi, and his star map was used there for centuries. In his famous *Book of Fixed Stars,* the scientist cataloged 1,018 stars according to their brightness, positions, and colors.

Al-Sufi also recorded the first celestial object outside our **galaxy** in the book. Al-Sufi described and drew what we today know is the Andromeda galaxy. He called it "a little cloud" lying before the mouth of an Arabic constellation named the Big Fish.

Al-Sufi used a tool called an **astrolabe** to locate stars and other celestial objects. The instrument has movable parts to set the time and date and gives the observer a picture of how the sky looks at his or her latitude. Al-Sufi wrote about the many possible uses of the astrolabe, including timekeeping and navigation.

Persian astronomer Abd al-Rahman al-Sufi.

the 16th century accepted his theories as fact. The name of his book, *The Almagest,* is not even a Greek word. It comes from the Arabic name *al-majisṭī,* which means "the greatest." Ninth-century Arab translations of Ptolemy's book fueled Islamic astronomy. Meanwhile, *The Almagest* remained lost to Europe until the Dark Ages ended.

One of the most important astronomers of this time was Abd al-Rahman al-Sufi. The Persian scientist spent years updating Ptolemy's star list for his own *Book of Fixed Stars.* Al-Sufi's star catalog named the stars differ-

ently than Ptolemy. The Greeks based star names on their constellations. An individual star might be referred to as "the top right star in constellation Lyra." Al-Sufi called this star Vega, giving each star its own Arabic name, separate from its constellation.

Many star names we use today are Arabic —Rigel, Fomalhaut, Aldebraran—and most

can be traced back to al-Sufi's book. One of the most unusual names is Betelgeuse, the reddish star in constellation Orion. Its original Arabic name was likely *Yad al-Jauzā,* but it got miscopied and repeatedly changed as it was translated from Arabic script to Medieval Latin and then to Italian and German.

This antique postcard shows the monument to Copernicus in Warsaw, Poland, built in 1830. *Library of Congress*

COPERNICAN REVOLUTION

News of Christopher Columbus landing on a continent unknown to Europe spread quickly—at least by 1492 standards. Nicolaus Copernicus was among the University of Kraków students amazed by the historic voyage. Europe's idea of the world was changing. But Copernicus would change the world's view of the universe itself.

Copernicus caught the astronomy bug while studying in Poland. He left to study church law in Italy but was lucky enough to get lodgings with the astronomy professor there. Astronomy was never Copernicus's profession, but it was his lifelong obsession. His day job was being a church business manager, called a canon, in a small town on the Baltic Sea. "This very remote corner of the Earth," is what Copernicus called what is today Frombork, Poland. Copernicus filled his free time with stargazing—and lots of reading.

Copernicus studied the texts of Ptolemy's ancient geocentric system. He read what the great thinkers and philosophers had written about it. Over the centuries, they'd added

Al-Sufi and the other Islamic astronomers believed they were fulfilling their creator's wishes. The Muslim holy book, the Qur'an, encourages exploring the universe, saying: "In the creation of the heavens and the earth . . . there are indeed signs for men of understanding." Apparently those signs did not include questioning the Ptolemaic system. Al-Sufi accepted that an unmoving Earth was at the universe's center because it meshed with Muslim beliefs. The Qur'an also states, "It is not for the Sun to overtake the Moon. . . . They all float, each in an orbit." It would be another five centuries before the Sun found its way to the center of things.

Make an Astrolabe

activity

Astrolabe means "star-taker," as in taking the measurement of the stars. It's an ancient instrument that measures the angles of space objects such as stars and planets above the horizon.

Take your own star measurements after making this simple astrolabe.

YOU'LL NEED

➡ String or heavy thread, 12 inches (30 cm) long

➡ Metal washer, bolt, or other weight

➡ Protractor, 6 inches (15 cm) with hole at the center

➡ Wide drinking straw

➡ Heavy tape

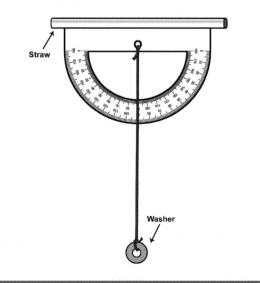

Straw

Washer

Horizon

1. Tie a washer or other weight to one end of the string.

2. Attach the other end of the string to the hole in the middle of the protractor's straight edge. Knot the string at the back of the protractor to hold it in the hole. If the hole is big, a bit of tape can help. Hold up the protractor, ruler side on top, and check that the string swings freely along the printed side of the protractor.

3. Set the straw against the ruler edge of the protractor and secure it there with tape. Your astrolabe is ready!

4. Test it out by using it to find your latitude. Find Polaris (see page 3) and then look at it through the straw. Note what degree the string lines up with on the protractor. (Your eye is at 0°.) Subtract that zenith angle from 90° to get your latitude. For example, if your astrolabe reads 42° with Polaris sighted (at zenith), then 90° − 42° = 48°.

5. Use your astrolabe to measure the latitude of the moon, planets, and stars. Make sure to write down the date and time with your measurements.

Nicolaus Copernicus (1473–1543)

Mikołaj Kopernik was born in Toruń, Poland. (Copernicus is the Latin version of his name.) He was the fourth child of a well-to-do mother and successful merchant father. When Copernicus was a young boy his father died, leaving his future in doubt. Fortunately, an uncle agreed to fund his education and eventually became the bishop who arranged for Copernicus's career as a church canon in Frombork.

Like many of the great Renaissance scientists, Copernicus had many interests. He was a mathematician, astronomer, law expert, physician, economist, and a speaker and translator of many languages. He was also an artist and painted his own portrait. Some historians think that it was Copernicus's artistic sense that drove him to put the Sun at the center. It was a more elegant, simple, aesthetically pleasing way for the universe to work.

A statue of Copernicus with a model of the Sun in the center of the universe. *Kumal*

Why create a Frankenstein if you don't need to? For Copernicus, the question of how celestial objects moved could be simply explained by putting the Sun in the center, with all of the planets—including a spinning Earth—orbiting around it.

Copernicus wrote up a brief, six-page leaflet introducing his Sun-centered, or **heliocentric**, ideas in 1514. He showed it to some friends but didn't publish it for nearly another three decades. Why? Maybe his job kept him too busy, or he couldn't stop fidgeting with details in the manuscript. Or perhaps Copernicus wanted to stay out of trouble. After all, the Church employed Copernicus. And the Church said that God created a unique Earth for mankind, so it should rightly be in the center of the universe. Earth wasn't like other planets! To think or say otherwise went against the Church, and was therefore heresy.

It was a young Austrian astronomy fan who finally talked Copernicus into going public. Georg Joachim Rheticus traveled to Frombork in 1539 after hearing rumors of Copernicus's work. Rheticus studied with Copernicus and convinced him to print his

odd bits and pieces to the Ptolemaic system in order to get it to match what they saw in the night sky. All of the ridiculously complicated circles inside orbits within spheres troubled Copernicus. All the added-on circles and adjusted orbits needed to explain

the Earth-centered system were to him like putting together a person from random feet, hands, and a head. "Since these fragments would not belong to one another at all, a monster rather than a man would be put together from them," Copernicus wrote.

book, *On the Revolutions of the Heavenly Spheres.* Four years later, Copernicus saw the final printed pages as he lay in bed. He'd had a stroke, and he died the same day. In his book, he summed up the logic of a heliocentric universe, writing, "In the midst of all dwells the Sun. For what better place could you find for the lamp in this exquisite temple, where it can illuminate everything at the same time?"

Of course, saying the Earth is not the center of the universe is one thing. Proving that our world is only one of the many planets that circle the Sun is quite another. That job would have to wait for someone else—and a new invention.

Get Ready to Star Watch
activity

Studying the stars isn't just for scientists. No matter where you live, there's something to see just by looking up at the night sky. Here are a few tips and tools to get you started.

➤➤ **Find some dark, open sky.** Rooftops, decks, and backyards are all great places. Too much light from streetlamps or houses can make stars harder to see.

➤➤ **Get comfortable.** A reclining lawn chair, sleeping pad, blanket, or exercise mat makes lying down while looking up a lot easier.

➤➤ **Eyes-only observations.** Don't worry about not having a telescope or binoculars at first. There's a lot to see with your own eyes. After all, that's how people have viewed stars for most of history. With the naked eye, you can likely see the **Milky Way**; moon craters; the planets Venus, Mercury, Jupiter, Mars, and Saturn; meteor showers; a few star clusters and nebulae; the Andromeda galaxy; dozens of constellations; and 2,000 to 3,000 different stars.

➤➤ **Create an observation notebook.** Having a notebook just for night-sky watching is helpful. It's a place to draw what you see, take notes, and jot down questions to research later. Some important things to note on each page: date and time, location, direction, and weather, as well as whether you're using binoculars, a telescope, or just your eyes.

➤➤ **Make an astronomy flashlight.** It takes a while for your eyes to adjust to seeing at night. Turning on a bright flashlight to write or check a chart can ruin your night vision! When stargazing, use a flashlight that glows with red light. It takes your eyes less time to recover night vision from red light. You can make a regular flashlight glow red by simply covering the lit end with red plastic wrap, red cellophane, a piece of transparent red report cover, or red tissue paper. Depending on its thickness, you can use a rubber band or strong tape to secure it. If your flashlight is small, painting the cover over the light with red nail polish can work, too.

➤➤ **Know the time, direction, and positions of stars.** A compass is helpful for recording directions in your notebook, and you should keep a watch for time. Websites (see page 119), books, or magazines that show the current month's star chart are helpful, too.

Galileo at his telescope.

2 1600s: Telescopes and Gravity

Winter nights are chilly for stargazing, even in Italy. Galileo Galilei must have felt the cold those December nights in 1610 when he began studying Venus. Or maybe the excitement of finally observing our neighbor planet through his **telescope** kept him warm.

Galileo had already been making discoveries with his telescope for more than a year. But he hadn't yet used the instrument to observe Venus, a planet known for thousands of years. The bright planet had been too close to the Sun to be seen well—until that winter. What the Italian physicist saw was well worth the wait. He peered through the telescope pointed toward Venus, sketching his observations night after night for many weeks.

After a few months, Galileo had a series of drawings with familiar shapes—half circles, crescent slivers, and bulging spheres. Venus has phases, like the moon. Galileo's discovery would prove Copernicus right.

SEEING THE SKIES

Venus is the brightest object in the sky after the Sun and the moon. It's often called the evening star or morning star. These names suit it, as Venus is brightest either right after sunset or just before sunrise. Venus is a familiar sight in the night sky—and was well known in Galileo's day. Galileo discovered, to everyone's surprise, that Venus has phases. Like the moon, the pattern of shadows on its surface changes. The illuminated part grows from a sliver to half to full and back again. Galileo saw what no one else could because he had a better view, thanks to a new-fangled invention: the telescope.

Galileo did not invent the telescope. A German-Dutch spectacles-maker did. Hans Lippershey applied for a patent in 1608 for a "device by means of which all things at a very great distance can be seen as if they were nearby." Basically, Lippershey figured out that looking through

Left: This engraving of Galileo's early telescopic observations shows the planets Saturn (top left), Jupiter (top middle), Mars (top right), and five different phases of Venus.

Right: One of the first telescopes made by Galileo. *NASA*

two different kinds of lenses, one in front of the other, created a kind of magnifying glass for distant objects. The invention was useful for seeing enemy ships, as well as peeping at neighbors.

When Galileo heard of the telescope, however, he knew it could be so much more. He turned a simple spyglass into the most important tool ever for astronomers.

The 45-year-old scientist was good with his hands. Over the years, Galileo had made many precise science instruments. He imme-

diately set out to build a better telescope with which to spy on the heavens. "And first I prepared a lead tube in whose ends I fitted two glasses, both [flat] on one side while the other side of one was spherically **convex** and of the other **concave**," Galileo wrote.

After a number of versions and "sparing neither labor nor expense," he constructed "an instrument so excellent that things seen through it appear about a thousand times larger and more than 30 times closer" than with the naked eye. Galileo put his most

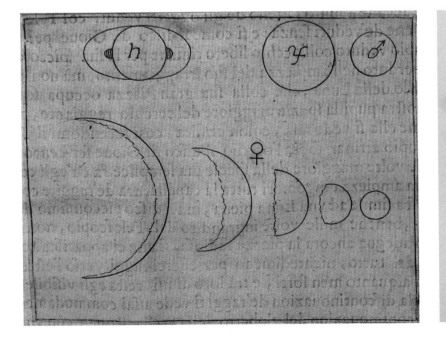

Changing Face of Venus

When Galileo turned his crude telescope toward Venus, he saw theory turn to proof. The shifting shapes he sketched of the shadowed and lit parts of our nearest neighbor planet changed with time. Venus has phases.

To Galileo this meant one thing: Venus is orbiting around the Sun, just like Earth is, only closer. He knew that only this heliocentric arrangement could create Venus's moonlike phases.

Heliocentric   Geocentric

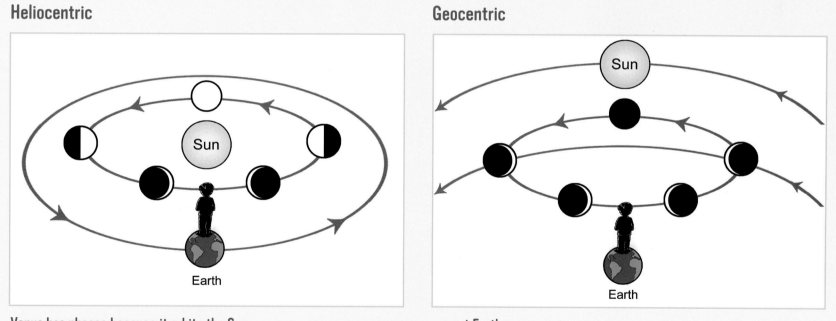

Venus has phases because it orbits the Sun . . .   . . . not Earth

In the Earth-centered system of Ptolemy, Venus traveled in a little circle between Earth and the Sun. In order for that to be true, the view of Venus from Earth would always be mostly in shadow, with only a lit crescent phase. But it isn't. Instead, Venus's surface is lit by a sun in the center of its orbit. This creates the dramatically changing phases we see from our viewpoint on Earth.

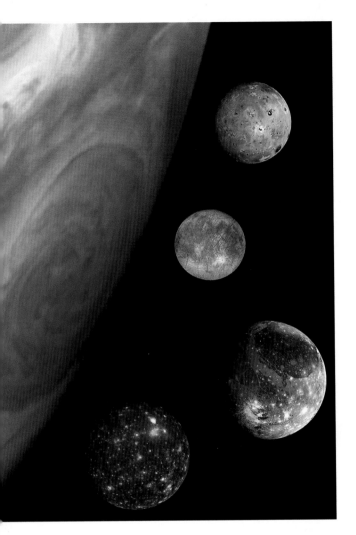

The four largest moons of Jupiter are called the Galilean moons, in their discoverer's honor. From top to bottom: Io, Europa, Ganymede, and Callisto. *NASA*

excellent instrument to work right away, aiming it up toward the night sky. What he observed changed the world's view of the universe and our place in it.

THE STARRY MESSENGER

The first thing Galileo observed was the moon. He did not see the perfectly smooth, glowing, magical, celestial sphere imagined by philosophers. Instead, he saw a world not unlike our own. "It is like the face of the Earth itself, which is marked here and there with chains of mountains and depths of valleys," he wrote.

In January 1610 Galileo extended his gaze, observing Jupiter. There he discovered the giant planet's four largest moons. Ours wasn't the only world orbited by moons! Earth wasn't so different from the celestial bodies, after all.

The telescope was revealing a much bigger heavenly realm, too. Galileo could tell that the stars he saw with his new tool were much farther away than the planets, and that there were many more stars than anyone had ever imagined. "To the three [stars] in Orion's belt and six in his sword that were observed

long ago, I have added eighty others seen recently," he wrote.

The more he looked, the more stars he saw. When Galileo steered his telescope toward the Milky Way, "truly unfathomable" numbers of stars popped into view. The Milky Way wasn't a heavenly cloud as many claimed. It was a frothy sea of stars. "For the Galaxy is nothing else than a [collection] of innumerable stars distributed in clusters," Galileo wrote. All these observations went into his quickly published book, *Starry Messenger*.

COPERNICUS, KEPLER, AND MYSELF

Galileo proudly wrote about the "great and very wonderful sights" his telescope revealed. He wasn't shy about it. The device got him a promotion and a raise in pay. But Galileo was also an insightful scientist. He knew that moons around Jupiter and the hordes of new stars were more than just amazing sights. All were evidence that the universe wasn't what most people thought it was. Galileo's observations showed that the Earth wasn't the center of everything. He explained in a letter that the planets circled the Sun, "something believed by the [ancient] Pythagoreans, Copernicus, Kepler, and myself, but not proved as it is now." The telescope provided proof.

The Kepler mentioned in the letter was Johannes Kepler, the greatest living astronomer at the time. Kepler was born in Germany. When Kepler was a sickly five-year-old boy in 1577, his mother pulled him from bed to see an astounding sight. The two trudged up a hill above town and peered into the winter night sky. Above was a bright star with a sparkling tail—a **comet**. Three years later, Katharine Kepler made sure her son saw an **eclipse** of the moon, too. She knew he was interested in how the world worked. Kepler would spend his life trying to figure out how all worlds worked.

Kepler and Galileo knew each other, though the two scientists never met in person. Everyone, Galileo included, knew that Kepler believed in a Sun-centered **cosmos** and a moving Earth. Kepler's 1596 book, *The Cosmographic Mystery,* defended Copernicus and his theory that the Earth spins and travels around the Sun once a year. Kepler even sent Galileo a copy, urging him in a letter to

The Power of Lenses

activity

A little telescope power can make a big difference in what's visible in the night sky. Want proof? Grab a pair of binoculars. Binoculars are like two mini telescopes—one for each eye. Find out how much more you can see while stargazing using a pair.

YOU'LL NEED

➺ Binoculars

➺ Your observation notebook (page 11)

➺ Sky-watching spot

1. Record what kind of binoculars you're using in your notebook. Binoculars have a two-part identification, for example 5 x 35 or 8 x 50. The first number is the magnification power. You'll see things five times closer with a 5-power pair of binoculars, eight times closer with an 8-power. The second number is the diameter (in millimeters) of the lens at the end of the binoculars. The bigger the diameter, the bigger the lens, and the more light it can gather. This is important for stargazing. You'll be able to see dimmer stars with an 8 x 50 pair than an 8 x 30. Both magnify to the same degree, but the larger lenses let in more starlight.

2. Get settled and comfortable and let your eyes adjust to the darkness. Choose a small section of the sky to observe. With just your eyes, sketch out what you can see in your notebook.

3. Using the binoculars, repeat step 2 with the same sky section. What more can you see? More stars, clearer craters, different objects, such as nebulae? Draw your new observations.

Galileo Galilei.

back him up as a fellow follower of Copernicus. "Would it not be much better to pull the wagon to its goal by our joint efforts. . . . Be of good cheer, Galileo, and come out publicly."

Galileo wasn't swayed. "Like you," he wrote Kepler, "I accepted the Copernican position several years ago." But Galileo was firm about holding his tongue. The risk was too great. "I would dare publish my thoughts if there were many like you; but, since there are not, I shall forebear."

PAPAL PROBLEMS

Galileo wouldn't be able to opt out for long. The situation in the Holy City of Rome was heating up. In February 1600, Church authorities arrested the philosopher Giordano Bruno. They charged him with heresy, stripped him naked, tied him to a stake, and burned him alive.

Making sure everyone followed Church rules was the job of the Inquisition. Those who went against Church doctrine were criminals, called heretics. Bruno had a long list of heretical beliefs, among them that Earth circled the Sun.

Galileo agreed with the ideas and theories in Copernicus's and Kepler's books. The heliocentric system made sense to the Italian physicist. But he didn't stick his neck out for the idea—at least not a first. That seemed to change after Galileo found proof of a Sun-centered cosmos with his telescopic discoveries. Maybe his own discoveries convinced him of it. Or perhaps he felt safe since fellow scientists were lauding his great discoveries. Galileo became quite famous. The most important scientist group in Italy invited him to join. Members wrote about the meeting in which Galileo demonstrated how the phases of Venus change as the planet circles the Sun. Such magnificent discoveries, they cried! Some in the Church supported Galileo, too. At least until newer leaders swept in a stricter view of holy scriptures.

By 1615 Galileo was under investigation by the Inquisition. Inquisitors claimed that the telescope was an evil device that made things appear in the sky that weren't really there at all. Galileo brashly responded by offering a reward of 10 times his annual salary to anyone who could make such a "magical" telescope.

Galileo was eventually arrested and put on trial for illegally teaching that the Earth moved. In 1633 he was convicted and banned from publishing scientific discoveries. He lived under house arrest for the final nine years of his life.

OVALS, NOT CIRCLES

Galileo was forced as an old man, under the threat of torture, to publicly reject what his own observations told him about the cosmos. But just because the law said the Earth was the center of universe didn't make it true. Support for the geocentric system was fading. Others were adding to the evidence supporting a Sun-centered system.

Johannes Kepler sorted out one of the long-debated problems with the **Copernican system**. Kepler was a student of Tycho Brahe, an amazing pre-telescope astronomer. Kepler knew firsthand from Brahe's precisely recorded observations how the planets moved across the sky over time. So why didn't these seen movements match Copernicus's theory of the planets orbiting the Sun in simple circles? Because their orbits aren't circular, Kepler discovered. The planets' paths around the Sun are oval-shaped, or **elliptical**.

This discovery became Kepler's first law of planetary motion. The other two laws describe how fast each planet travels in its orbit and how that speed depends on the path's size. Kepler's laws perfectly predicted where, when, and how planets move across the sky.

Watching and tracking the planets proves all three of Kepler's laws of planetary motion. But observation doesn't explain *why* planets move that way. Why do planets have

Galileo Galilei (1564–1642)

Galileo was the oldest son of an important Italian musician, Vincenzo Galilei. As a teenager, Galileo was on the path to priesthood. But he switched to a university to study medicine where he fell in love with mathematics and started making scientific discoveries. By showing that careful experiments, observations, and mathematical calculations could explain how nature worked, Galileo became the first modern scientist and helped debunk the myths of medieval science as part of Europe's Renaissance.

Galileo's discoveries about **inertia**, flotation, and falling bodies, among others, were the beginning of the scientific study of motion.

As an astronomer he made many discoveries about our solar system and beyond. Galileo studied the Sun and **sunspots**, showing our sun as a changing star. Some historians believe his time studying the Sun likely caused his eventual blindness.

Galileo's discoveries with the telescope gave proof to supporters of the Copernican heliocentric system. Unfortunately, it also landed him in trouble with the Catholic Church. The scientist lived under house arrest for the rest of his life after his heresy conviction. In 1992 Pope John Paul II exonerated Galileo, 350 years after the scientist's death.

elliptical orbits? And why do they speed up when they are closer to the Sun? Kepler thought maybe some kind of magnetic push and pull between celestial objects could be at work. But he didn't figure out what power or force kept the planets circling the Sun. That mystery would remain for a future generation to solve.

Johannes Kepler (1571–1630)

Johannes Kepler was a German astronomer. He became a fan of Copernicus's Sun-centered theory in college. Kepler taught math and astronomy before becoming an assistant to the great Danish astronomer Tycho Brahe (1546–1601). Kepler made improvements to the telescope, too, using two convex lenses that allowed a wider, brighter (though upside-down) view.

Kepler's discovery that the planets move in elliptical orbits led to Kepler's three laws of planetary motion, which state:

1. All the planets follow an elliptical orbit around the Sun.
2. The planets move faster when they are closer to the Sun.
3. Each planet's orbit time is related mathematically to its distance from the Sun.

Kepler wrote the following epitaph for himself: "I used to measure the heavens, now I shall measure the shadows of the earth. Although my soul was from heaven, the shadow of my body lies here."

THE GRAVITY OF IT ALL

The year Galileo died in Italy, a young widow named Hannah Ayscough Newton gave birth to a baby boy in England. Isaac Newton would grow up to be a great scientist, one who would again change how people saw and understood the universe.

Newton's teachers didn't think much of him as a young boy. He seemed to like tinkering with gadgets more than studying. Young Isaac built a small grain-grinding windmill and a clock powered by dripping water. But his mother was so unimpressed with his grades that she pulled 14-year-old Newton out of school. Better to put him to work managing the farm, she thought. Apparently, the hard labor didn't suit teenage Newton. Within a few years he was back in school, this time studying hard. He soon went on to Cambridge University.

Newton found himself back on his family's estate in 1666. An outbreak of the Plague was attacking Cambridge and its residents. Twenty-four-year-old Newton fled town to avoid the dangerous disease. The story goes that while kicking back in the country, a falling apple caught Newton's eye. Watching the red fruit fall from its tree to the ground got him thinking. A force had pulled the apple downward toward Earth. Was that force the same as the force that keeps the moon in its orbit? The same as what pulls Earth around the Sun?

The falling apple story may or may not be true, but something got young Newton thinking about why moons and planets orbit. What he came up with was **gravity**. Objects in space attract each other. In fact, there is a force of attraction among all **matter** everywhere. That force is called universal gravitation, or gravity.

Newton published his ideas about gravity in his 1687 book *Principia*. In the book, Newton laid out gravity's rules: all bodies in the universe attract one another across space; the force of gravity depends on how much **mass** those bodies have and the distance between them. That's pretty much it. Objects that are far apart have less gravitational attraction to each other than objects that are close together. And more massive objects create a greater gravitational force of attraction than smaller ones.

"Kepler's laws," wrote Newton, "are sufficiently near to the truth to have led to the discovery of the law of attraction of the bodies of the solar system." Newton's law of universal gravitation explained why planets move like they do. Orbits are squashed into ovals, or ellipses, because the Sun not only pulls on the planets, the planets pull on the Sun, too, stretching the orbiting circles into ovals. And planets speed up when they orbit closer to the Sun because of the difference in distance. Gravity makes it all work.

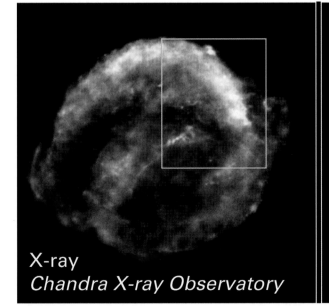

X-ray
Chandra X-ray Observatory

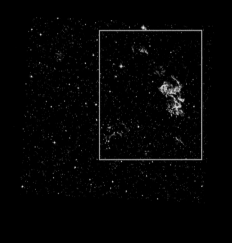

Visible
Hubble Space Telescope

In 1604 Johannes Kepler saw a star explode in the night sky. He noted the observation, so the supernova was later named after him. Newer telescopes can now study in great detail what's left of the explosion.

NASA/ESA/Johns Hopkins University

A replica of Isaac Newton's 1672 reflecting telescope.

Andrew Dunn

Make a Reflecting Telescope

activity

*Galileo's **refracting telescope** used a convex lens to bend, or refract, light. Newton's **reflecting telescope** instead bounces, or reflects, light off a concave mirror. The concave primary mirror focuses the light onto a flat secondary mirror that reflects the image up into an eyepiece for viewing.*

You can make your own simple reflecting telescope to find out how mirrors magnify starlight.

YOU'LL NEED

⇒ Concave magnifying mirror (such as a magnifying makeup mirror)

⇒ Measuring tape

⇒ Heavy white paper or poster board

⇒ Flashlight or reading lamp

⇒ Heavy tape

⇒ Modeling clay or putty

⇒ 1-inch (2.5-cm) square flat mirror

⇒ Protractor

⇒ Small magnifying lens

⇒ Cardboard shipping tube or poster board

⇒ 2 small cardboard tubes or posterboard

⇒ Scissors

⇒ Double-sided tape

⇒ Chopstick with flat edges

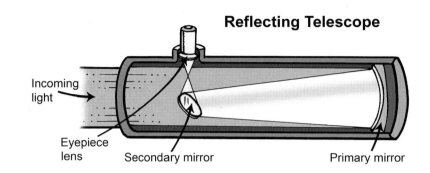

Reflecting Telescope

Incoming light

Eyepiece lens

Secondary mirror

Primary mirror

1. Measure the focal length of your concave magnifying mirror. This is the distance between the mirror and where its curvature brings the rays of light to a focused point. Set a piece of white poster board or paper next to a bright flashlight or reading lamp in a darkened room, as shown. Create a stripe across the light by covering the center of the light with a thin strip of heavy tape. Hold your concave magnifying mirror facing the lamp and move it until it reflects the light onto the paper. Move the mirror closer and farther from the paper until the stripe sharply focuses. Measure the distance between the mirror and the light and write it down—this is the focal length. Next, measure and write down the mirror's diameter.

2. Test out your combination of lens and mirrors before going on. Set up a tubeless telescope. On a flat surface, use some modeling clay to stand the concave mirror on end. Subtract the mirror's diameter from the focal length you measured, then place the small secondary flat mirror at that distance from the concave mirror. Use the protractor to set it at a 45° angle and hold it in place with the clay.

3. Hold a magnifying lens above the secondary mirror and look down through it to the small mirror. Can you see what's reflected from the

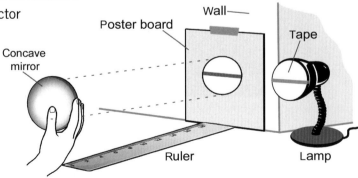

Wall

Poster board

Tape

Concave mirror

Ruler

Lamp

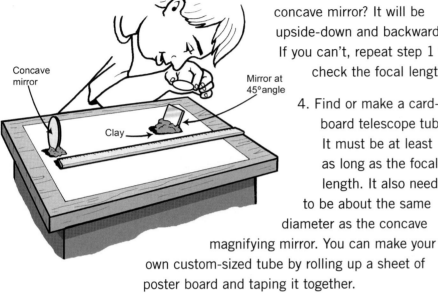

Concave mirror

Clay

Mirror at 45° angle

concave mirror? It will be upside-down and backward. If you can't, repeat step 1 to check the focal length.

4. Find or make a cardboard telescope tube. It must be at least as long as the focal length. It also needs to be about the same diameter as the concave magnifying mirror. You can make your own custom-sized tube by rolling up a sheet of poster board and taping it together.

5. Tape the concave magnifying mirror to one end of the tube so that its reflecting surface faces inside.

6. Subtract the diameter of the concave magnifying mirror from its focal length, as you did in step 2. Measure this distance from the concave mirror and mark it in several places around the tube. Connect the marks so there's a line all the way around the tube. Is your tube a lot longer than this mark? It only needs to be a few inches longer, so you can cut it down if desired. Set it aside.

7. Cut along the entire length of one of the smaller cardboard tubes. Remember, you can also make a tube by rolling up some poster board.

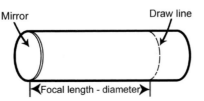

Mirror

Draw line

Focal length - diameter

8. Set the magnifying lens on a flat surface. Hold the cut-open tube so one end covers up the magnifying lens. Squeeze the tube until it tightly grips the lens, then tape it closed so it keeps this width. Attach the lens to one end of the tube with tape. This is the eyepiece.

9. Repeat step 7 with the other small tube. Fit this tube over the end of the eyepiece with the lens. Squeeze and slide the loose outer tube until it fits snugly over the eyepiece tube. It needs to be able to slide but also stay in place without slipping down. Tape the outer tube closed so it keeps this width.

10. Slide out the eyepiece and set it aside. Place the outer small tube on top of the telescope tube where you drew the line. Position the tube so that it evenly straddles the line. Trace the bottom of the small tube onto the large one. Cut out the hole you traced. Set the outer small tube into it, adjusting the hole as necessary, securing with tape.

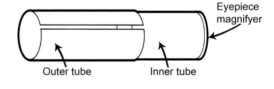

Eyepiece magnifyer

Outer tube

Inner tube

11. Wrap the measuring tape around the telescope tube to measure its circumference. Divide it by 2. Mark off the start and end of this distance along the line that wraps around the large tube that now has a hole it in. The idea is to have two points evenly spaced from both sides of the hole along the line.

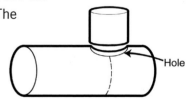

Hole

CONTINUED ON PAGE 24 . . .

. . . CONTINUED FROM PAGE 23

activity

12. Poke small holes at the two points and then push a chopstick in one hole, through the tube, and out the other hole.

13. Place double-sided tape on the back of the flat mirror. Reach down through the hole and stick the mirror to one of the edges

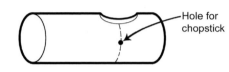

Hole for chopstick

of the chopstick inside the tube. Turn the chopstick from the outside so it's at a 45° angle. This is the secondary mirror that will collect the focused light and bounce it up to the eyepiece.

14. Slip the eyepiece into place, lens-end side down.

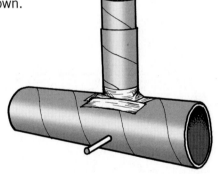

15. Test it out! Set a small flashlight in front of the telescope. Place your hand a few inches above the eyepiece to see if the light correctly bounces up and out onto your palm. If not, try focusing the eyepiece by sliding it in and out and rotating the chopstick to move the secondary mirror.

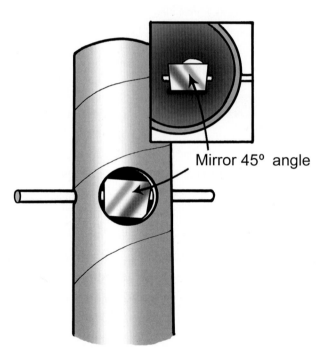

Mirror 45° angle

BOUNCE, NOT BEND

Figuring out that the same force that pulls a dropped stone to the ground also keeps the planets in orbit wasn't Newton's only accomplishment. He pretty much revolutionized **physics** in every way—and invented calculus. Light was another of his subjects. Newton's work with light led to an important tool for astronomers. He invented a new kind of telescope—a kind much better for stargazing.

Galileo's telescope was a narrow metal tube with a lens inside it at each end. The end you looked through had an **eyepiece lens**. It was concave, or curved inward, like a bowl. On the other end of the tube was the **objective lens**. It was convex, or curved outward. This combination of lenses magnified well, but had what's called a very small field of view. Using a Galilean telescope, you'd only be able to look at a quarter of the moon at one time.

Johannes Kepler fixed this by designing a telescope with both a convex objective lens and an eyepiece lens. His telescope flipped things upside down, making it not so great as a spyglass. But it had a larger field of view.

Statue of Isaac Newton in the chapel of Trinity College, Cambridge. *Andrew Dunn*

You could see the whole moon at once with Kepler's telescope.

Early telescopes also created distracting halos of colored light. The rough edges of the lenses acted like tiny **prisms**, splitting light into a rainbow around the image. While studying light, Isaac Newton used prisms to purposely break up white light into colors.

Newton used his discovery to improve the telescope. A mirror reflects light, bouncing it away. But a mirror with a curved, concave shape bounces the reflected light to a point of focus, just like a lens. Newton figured out that swapping the lenses with curved mirrors got rid of the rainbow halo. Newton himself fashioned the tube and cast and polished the metal mirror for his invention. Those childhood years tinkering had made him handy.

It was the first reflecting telescope. (Galileo's was a refracting telescope.) Newton's first telescope was only 6 inches (15 cm) long and its main mirror just 1 inch (2.5 cm) wide. But the telescope was so powerful that he could clearly see the planets in detail like never before. "If I have seen further it is by standing on the shoulders of giants," Newton wrote. Seeing further was exactly what reflecting telescopes did for astronomy. And seeing further meant seeing things no one even knew existed—yet.

Sir Isaac Newton (1642–1727)

Isaac Newton was one of the greatest scientists of all time. He changed how we saw the world in very fundamental ways. The English scientist and mathematician discovered gravity, invented calculus, dissected light itself, and invented the reflecting telescope, all in the space of two years! His laws of motion are still used today to describe and predict everything from how a rocket launches to how much weight a bridge can hold up.

Newton was born after his father's death. His childhood was difficult and he lived much of it with his grandparents. Newton attended and then taught at Cambridge University in England.

It took Newton 20 years to share his findings. Another famous astronomer, Edmond Halley, talked him into it and paid for the publication of *Principia*. It is still considered one of the most important books in the history of science. It included Newton's theory of universal gravitation and was the first book showing that the same scientific principles apply everywhere—on Earth or out in the heavens.

Newton experimenting with light.

Split White Light

activity

The first **spectroscopes** used prisms to separate white light into colors. A glass prism's flat sides bend, or refract, light waves according to their **wavelengths**, splitting light into its component rainbow of colors.

Modern spectroscopes use what's called a **diffraction grating** to do the same. Most have tiny parallel ridges that bend and split light into a thin rainbow of colors. Have you ever noticed that the backs of music and computer CDs often have a rainbow sheen to them? The information on a CD is recorded by a laser, which burns tiny parallel grooves into the plastic creating a diffraction grating.

You can use a CD to split some light, too.

YOU'LL NEED

➡ Aluminum foil

➡ Flashlight

➡ Rubber band or tape

➡ Pushpin

➡ Used music or computer CD (hint: a blank CD doesn't work as well)

1. Cover a flashlight with aluminum foil and secure it with a rubber band, or tape.

2. Use the pushpin to poke a small hole in the foil over the flashlight's center.

3. Go someplace dim, away from lights and windows. Shine the flashlight at the back of the CD. Move the CD and flashlight until you get the right angle that reveals a very slender, straight column of rainbow light. This is the light of the flashlight's spectrum.

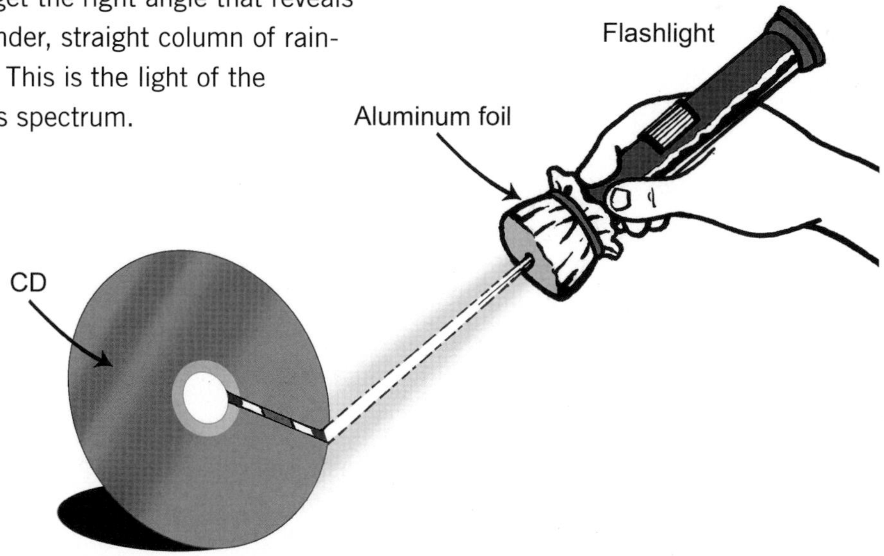

Flashlight

Aluminum foil

CD

Visitors to the Herschel Museum in Bath, England, can still see some of the floor stones cracked by the furnace accident.

Mick Hyde

3 1700s–1915: Unveiling the Stars

William Herschel knew there was a problem the instant he saw the shiny drops. The beads of melted metal were dripping down from the bottom of his furnace. The ovenlike furnace melted solid pieces of tin and copper into a hot batter of metal, but it shouldn't be leaking it onto the floor. There must be a crack in the furnace, thought Herschel. And there were more than 500 pounds of metal above the crack.

Just as he realized that this batch of metal would never become a telescope mirror, the heat and weight of it split the furnace bottom open. Liquid metal gushed out onto the basement floor stones, exploding them like boiling water tossed on ice. "Both my brothers . . . were obliged to run out at opposite doors," wrote Caroline Herschel of the accident. "For the stone flooring . . . flew about in all directions as high as the ceiling." The Herschels bolted from the basement, collapsing from heat and exhaustion once outside. Astronomy can be dangerous. Or, at least, telescope making in 1781 was.

Telescopes are all about collecting faraway light. The bigger the telescope, the more light it can gather. William Herschel wanted to zoom in on the faintest lights in the night sky. The astronomer wanted to see what could be found farther out in the darkness. To do that he needed better telescopes with bigger mirrors, so he became an expert telescope maker.

As the story of the exploding floor proves, it wasn't easy work. Even when the metal was successfully mixed, melted, and poured into a mold, hours of grinding were needed to shape and polish the metal disc into a mirror. William's sister Caroline would read to and care for her older brother as he sat working nonstop for up to 16 hours at a time, steadily polishing a mirror. "By way of keeping him alive, I was constantly obliged to feed him by putting the victuals by bits into his mouth," she wrote.

MUSICAL BEGINNINGS

It was not a life these siblings would have imagined for themselves growing up. William was born Friedrich Wilhelm Herschel in Hanover, Germany. His father was a musician for the army, and young Friedrich Wilhelm

William and Caroline Herschel at work.

In this engraving of an elderly William Herschel is the part of the constellation Gemini in which he discovered Uranus.

and became a successful music teacher and performer.

Caroline Herschel was 22 when she moved to Bath, England, where her older brother was then working as a chapel organist. She left Germany to keep house for William and sing in his choir, but her time was quickly overtaken with his new obsession. After reading about telescopes, William Herschel was hooked. "I was so delighted with the subject that I wished to see the heavens & planets with my own eyes thro' one of the instruments," he wrote. Caroline Herschel was soon as entranced with the stars as her brother. She became an amazing astronomer, too, making many discoveries. Together, the Herschels founded modern astronomy.

William and Caroline Herschel spent the rest of their lives systematically mapping and cataloging all the stars they could see—more than 90,000. Every clear night, even in winter, the pair surveyed the sky. When the Sun was up, Caroline wrote up their findings and William improved their sky gazing tools. Armed with William's ever-bigger, ever-better telescopes, the sibling astronomers charted thousands of never-before-seen

learned to play the oboe, violin, piano, and other instruments.

Teenage Friedrich Wilhelm also joined a military band with his brother, but he didn't like the life of a soldier musician in wartime. Tired of bloody battlefields and nights sleeping in ditches, Wilhelm escaped to England at 19. There he changed his name to William

William and Caroline Herschel

William Herschel (1738–1822) and Caroline Lucretia Herschel (1750–1848) were brother and sister astronomers, both born in Germany. William Herschel is often considered the founder of modern stellar (star) astronomy. He also discovered the seventh planet, Uranus.

William Herschel was a musician by trade, only becoming interested in astronomy in middle age. A brilliant craftsman, he became the master telescope maker of his time. His discovery in 1781 of Uranus with his homemade reflecting telescopes earned him fame and a paid position as royal astronomer to King George III, who also gave Caroline Herschel an annual pension as her brother's assistant.

The pair became full-time professional astronomers. Caroline was a great hunter of comets, discovering eight herself, as well as identifying three new nebulae.

William Herschel was knighted in 1816. His gravestone reads (in Latin): "He broke through the barriers of the heavens."

William Herschel's son, John Herschel (1792–1871), was also an important astronomer. John Herschel studied **binary stars** like his father, made the first telescopic study of the Southern Hemisphere **starscape**, and pioneered the use of photography as a tool in astronomy.

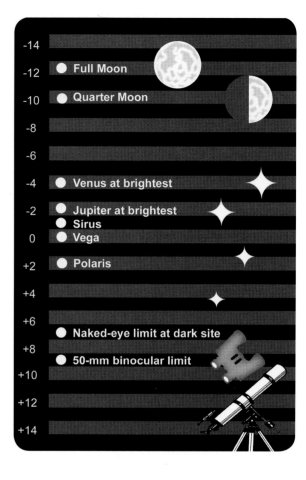

The ancient Greeks used a 1-to-6 scale to describe how bright a star looked in the night sky. The lower the magnitude number, the brighter the star.

stars. And they made many amazing discoveries in the process.

Finding a seventh planet, Uranus, in 1781 is perhaps the most famous Herschel discovery. But investigating what was beyond our small solar system was what really interested them.

Part of the Herschels' cataloging included noting how bright a star looks—its magnitude. The 1-to-6 star magnitude scale was invented by the ancient Greeks. Magnitude 6 stars are the faintest able to be seen with the naked eye. A magnitude 1 star is 100 times brighter than a magnitude 6. So, the lower the magnitude number, the easier a star is to see because it's brighter.

By surveying the stars over time, William Herschel found some stars that changed

Make a 3-D Starscape

activity

Constellations are star patterns in Earth's dome of night sky. But constellations are artificial groupings. They don't really exist out in space. The individual stars that make up constellations are actually at vastly different distances from Earth and are often very far apart. Give yourself a different view of a famous constellation in this activity.

YOU'LL NEED

➡ Enlarged copy of Orion pattern

➡ Styrofoam produce tray or piece of corrugated cardboard

➡ Glue

➡ Sheet of black paper

➡ Pushpin

➡ 7 pieces of fishing line or heavy thread, 18 inches (46 cm) long

➡ Tape

➡ Beads, washers, or hex nuts

➡ Ruler or tape measure

➡ Pen

➡ Scissors

1. Create a larger version of the seven-star pattern of Orion. You can enlarge the image with a photocopier, or simply trace and then redraw the simple seven-star pattern. Make the pattern as large as you can and still fit it on a foam tray or piece of corrugated cardboard. Only the area of the pattern with stars needs to fit, basically the hunter's shoulders to knees—the entire drawing of the ancient hunter for whom the constellation is named isn't necessary.

2. Glue the Orion pattern to one side of the foam tray or cardboard. Glue the black paper to the other side.

3. Use the pushpin to carefully poke small holes where each of the seven stars appear on the pattern. Go all the way through the tray or cardboard and the black paper.

4. Thread a piece of fishing line up through one of the star holes you just punched. Knot it and tape it down onto the pattern if necessary. Repeat until all seven star holes have fishing line hanging down below them.

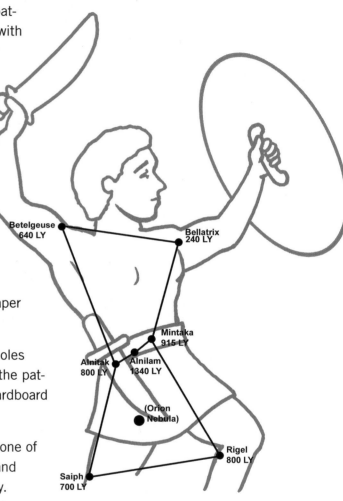

Orion Constellation Star Name	Distance from Earth in Light-Years	String Distance in Inches (Centimeters)
Betelgeuse	640	6.5 (16)
Bellatrix	240	2.5 (6)
Alnitak	800	8 (20)
Alnilam	1,340	13.5 (34)
Mintaka	915	9 (23)
Saiph	700	7 (18)
Rigel	800	8 (20)

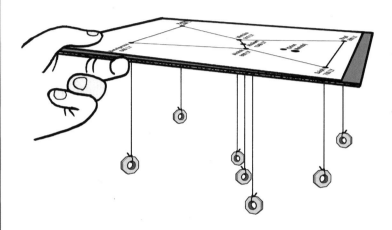

5. Gather up your seven "stars." Choose beads, washers, or hex nuts that are heavy enough to pull the string you're using taut. Use the table above to figure out where to tie on each bead or nut. For example, Rigel is 800 **light-years** away, which is represented by 8 inches (20 cm). Measure 8 inches from the black paper along Rigel's length of fishing line. Mark it with a pen. Then tie the bead onto the line at the 8-inch mark and trim off the extra. Repeat until all seven have stars hanging. (If you've got star stickers, you can stick them onto the beads or hex nuts.)

6. Have a friend hold the starry mobile so it's even and the stars hang down without tangling. Now look at Orion from all angles and sides, including from underneath.

Think about it: How is each view different? Which is the one we see in the winter sky?

Messier's Catalog

Charles Messier (1730–1817) caught comet fever at the age of 14 when he saw his first one shining in the night sky. The Frenchman went on to become a comet hunter, discovering 13.

While searching for comets, the astronomer became irritated by objects that looked a bit like faraway comets but weren't. So he listed them all in a catalog so others wouldn't confuse them with comets. His 1784 *Catalogue of Nebulae and Star Clusters* included 103 nebulae, galaxies, and star clusters.

Most of these objects Messier discovered himself and are still called Messier Objects. Messier 45 (or M45) is the Pleiades star cluster, for example, and the Andromeda spiral galaxy is Messier 31 (M31).

their brightness, called **variable stars**. It was more evidence that the star field we see isn't an unchanging shell around our solar system. Stars came in different kinds. Add to that more than 800 double stars that were charted by the Herschels. These binary stars orbit around each other. It was more proof that stars aren't stuck in one place, and that Newton's law of gravity also ruled the distant heavens.

MILKY GALAXY

Eventually William Herschel's telescopes saw more stars than any instruments ever built. In 1784 the Herschels turned their attention to the brilliant band of stars that stretch from horizon to horizon across the night sky.

The Milky Way was named by the Greeks, who thought the cloudy swath looked like spilled milk. Thanks to Galileo's earlier observations, 18th-century astronomers knew that a great concentration of stars made up the Milky Way. But no one knew its real shape—or what it really was.

William Herschel changed that when he assigned himself a massive task. He decided to count all the stars he could see in a circle all around him. Herschel was known to say, "The undevout astronomer must be mad."

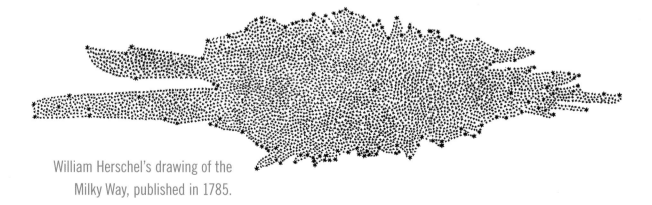

William Herschel's drawing of the Milky Way, published in 1785.

The stars revealed their secrets only to those willing to put in the telescope time. By counting the stars, measuring their motions, and doing some math, Herschel made the first map of the Milky Way. He claimed it was not simply a band of thickly concentrated stars, but that it was in fact a vast disc of stars—a galaxy in today's terms.

The stars in the Milky Way appear so thick because we're inside of the galaxy, looking out to the rim of it all around us. Imagine being the hub of a wheel and seeing the tire all around you. Our planet circling the Sun is a tiny dustlike speck within the disc of the Milky Way. Our solar system is just one tiny island in the galaxy. Herschel believed this Milky Way was all there was, the entire universe. And to him its dimensions seemed enormous and the distances between the stars incredibly vast.

FINDING A PROJECT

William Huggins was a wealthy young man. Like other Englishmen of his social class, he enjoyed the hobby of astronomy. Many upper-class homes had small telescopes. Looking at the moon and planets was a fashionable pastime during the Victorian age.

Huggins purchased his first telescope at age 18. It cost a steep £15, about a year's earnings for a laborer in 1842. Huggins didn't study astronomy in college. In fact, he left his studies early to help run the family drapery business. The London-based business did well, and Huggins kept up his interest in optical instruments—both telescopes and microscopes. However, Huggins yearned to be a serious scientist. He was determined to find a way to make a name for himself as a true contributor to the sciences.

At age 30, William Huggins sold his business and house in London. He purchased

A more modern panoramic view of the Milky Way. *2MASS/J. Carpenter, T. H. Jarrett, & R. Hurt*

Milky Way on Edge activity

What's the shape of the Milky Way? If you said spiral shaped, you're right. If you said band or ribbon shaped, you're right, too. The Milky Way is a spiral galaxy, but there's no way to see that spiral shape from here, inside the galaxy. Think about it: you can't see the shape of a tree if you're sitting on one of its limbs!

The Milky Way looks brightest to us as a band across the sky when we look in the direction of greatest concentration of stars. This is a view through an edge of the galaxy's disc. See the difference your angle of view makes in this activity.

YOU'LL NEED

➡ Flat piece of clear plastic (photo holder, ruler, etc.)

➡ Light source (small lamp, wide flashlight)

➡ Heavy-duty aluminum foil

➡ Craft knife

➡ Old magazine for cutting surface

➡ Adult helper

➡ Clear tape

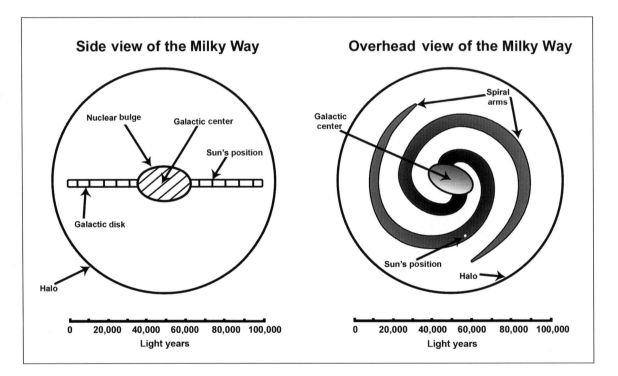

1. Start by choosing a piece of plastic and a light source that will work together. The plastic needs to sit on top of the light and completely cover it, but shouldn't hang over the light too much.

2. Use the plastic piece as a pattern and cut out a sheet of aluminum foil its exact size. Then lay the foil square on an old magazine or other safe cutting surface. With an adult's help, carefully cut some lines into the foil without reaching the edge of it, as shown. You can arrange the slices into a spiral or pinwheel shape, but it's not necessary.

3. Use tape to attach the foil to one side of the plastic piece. Use as much tape as needed to get the aluminum to lie directly on the plastic.

4. Turn off any lights in the room and turn on the light source. First look at the galaxy from overhead, looking down to see the whole spiral or sliced area. Then look at it on edge, seeing the light coming through only the sides of the plastic. Which view is more like our view of the Milky Way in the sky? Which is brighter?

Cut outs in foil

Aluminum foil taped over clear plastic

Wide flashlight or light

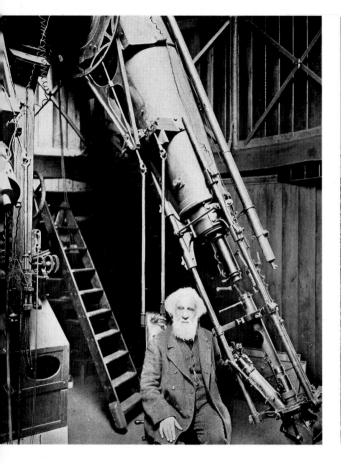

William Huggins inside his observatory, and what it looked like from outside.

above the ground. This meant the neighboring houses wouldn't block the view. Inside the deluxe observatory was an astronomical clock and telescopes that were mounted on concrete pillars to prevent shaking. Huggins topped his observatory with a domed roof that opened to the night sky.

William Huggins was then a full-time astronomer with a state-of-the-art private observatory. He enthusiastically titled his early notebook *Phenomena Observed by Will. Huggins through his Telescope* and got to work. Huggins began filling notebooks with observations of the planets and their surfaces.

But this was work other amateurs were already doing. "I soon became a little dissatisfied with the routine character of ordinary astronomical work," wrote Huggins. "I sought about in my mind for the possibility of research upon the heavens in a new direction or by new methods." So in 1858 Huggins traded up for a bigger, better telescope in hopes of equipping himself for more serious work: observing beyond the planets. Surely there was something out in the universe that still needed discovering!

a small home farther from the smoggy city center, one that sat on higher ground. It was a better site for what Huggins had decided to do: build an observatory. Carpenters built onto the house directly off the second floor by planting iron pillars into the ground. The observatory would be raised 16 feet (5 m)

Handy Sky Distances

Have you ever tried to point out a star or planet in the night sky to someone else? It can be difficult to describe which tiny point of light you want them to see. Stargazers and sky watchers use a simple system of measurement in degrees to describe positions of stars and other objects in the night sky.

Think of the sky as a giant dome overhead. All half circles (think of a protractor) go from 0° to 180°, with 90° at the top. The highest point is the top of the half circle at 90° and is called the *zenith*. The horizon is the bottom, straight edge of the dome floor. So if someone says the constellation is 45° above the northern horizon, you'd look north, and then about halfway between the horizon and zenith.

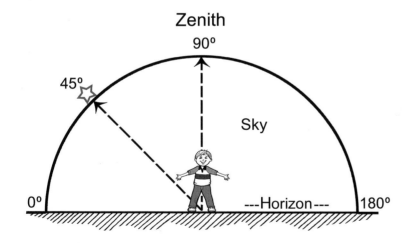

For smaller distances, such as those between stars, you've already got a "handy" tool for estimating degrees: your hand can be used as a protractor of sorts. With your arm outstretched, the distance in degrees from the tip of your pinky to tip of your thumb is about 20°, the width of your fist is about 10°, three fingers across is about 5°, and a pinky is about 1° thick.

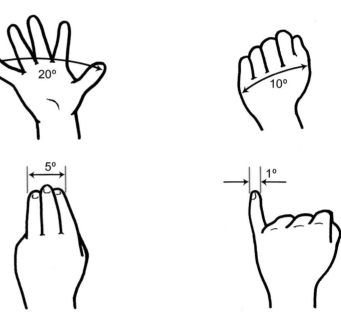

Test it out for yourself the next time you're outside at night. Here are some easy-to-find measurements:

Big Dipper: 5° between two "pouring edge" stars, 20° from end to end

Polaris: 30° from North Star to closest star in Big Dipper

Great Square of Pegasus: each side is about 15° wide

Andromeda Galaxy: 1° wide

Orion's Belt: 2.5° wide

How Far to a Star?

Just how far away are the stars? This question was first answered by a German accountant. Friedrich Bessel (1784–1846) did such a good job teaching himself astronomy that the king gave him his own new observatory at Königsberg. There, along the Baltic Sea, Bessel watched a pair of stars through his telescope. The faint but nearby stars were called 61 Cygni.

Bessel was trying to measure the distance to 61 Cygni from Earth using **parallax**. You can see how parallax works yourself. Just set an object—say, a soda can—a couple of feet away from you. Staring at the can, alternately close your right and left eye. The can will appear to jump sideways against the background. The jump appears because your eyes are a few inches apart, so the left eye sees the can from a slightly different angle than the right eye.

To create this change in angle when viewing from Earth, astronomers look at a star at different times of the year when Earth is in a different position in its orbit around the Sun. Measuring how much the star shifted between, for example, January and July, and knowing the **diameter** of Earth's orbit, lets you calculate the distance from Earth to that star.

And this is why Friedrich Bessel spent so much time looking at 61 Cygni. He carefully measured its position in the sky over several years. In 1838 he had it. The star system was 60,000,000,000,000 miles away (96,000,000,000,000 km). Today, we'd say 11.4 light-years. Bessel became the first person to measure the distance from Earth to a star.

SPLITTING SUNLIGHT

By Huggins's time, astronomers had discovered and mapped thousands of stars. But no one knew much about them. Early 19th-century astronomers knew that stars were hot objects, were very far away, and were not all the same. That was about it. What stars were made of, where they came from, and what made them different were mysteries. Those mysteries were solved by splitting light into separate colors.

Light is what astronomers crave. Nearly every discovery about the universe has come from different ways of studying light—whether it's glowing from a star or reflecting off a planet. Figuring out how to see and study the kinds of light from stars would reveal their distances, sizes, colors, temperatures—and tell their life stories.

The science of splitting light is called **spectroscopy**. Isaac Newton started it when he used a glass prism to separate sunlight into a rainbow. Each color of light has its own wavelength, so it bends differently when passing through a prism. Light with longer wavelengths (such as red or orange) bends the least, while light of shorter wavelengths (such as purple or blue) bends more. Dividing light by its wavelengths creates a **spectrum**, a band of light separated into colors. A rainbow is a spectrum, for example.

In 1819 a German optician named Joseph von Fraunhofer invented the spectroscope, an instrument that splits light with a prism and then spreads out the spectra into wide bands of separated colors for study. Scientists were puzzled by these newfangled spectra. Sunlight through a spectroscope makes a rainbow, but adds in black lines near where the colors change. What could be causing these "Fraunhofer lines"?

The question wouldn't be answered for decades, and not until scientists discovered that chemicals and wavelengths of light are connected. If you've watched a fireworks display, you've seen evidence of this connection. It's the different chemical ingredients that give fireworks their many colors. A chemical element produces light of a specific wavelength when it's heated, creating a color. Sodium burns yellow, burning copper has a green flame, and potassium is purple.

Knowing what pattern the spectrum of each element creates turns out to be useful. Spectroscopy today is still used to find out what's in all kinds of unknown substances. (Think crime scene forensics and airport screening.) Spectroscopy also explains those dark Fraunhofer lines in sunlight spectra. They are also created by the chemicals in their source—our sun. From the Sun's spectra, scientists were able to determine what elements our Sun is composed of.

STUDYING STARLIGHT

"This news was to me like the coming upon a spring of water in a dry and thirsty land," William Huggins wrote. He had his project

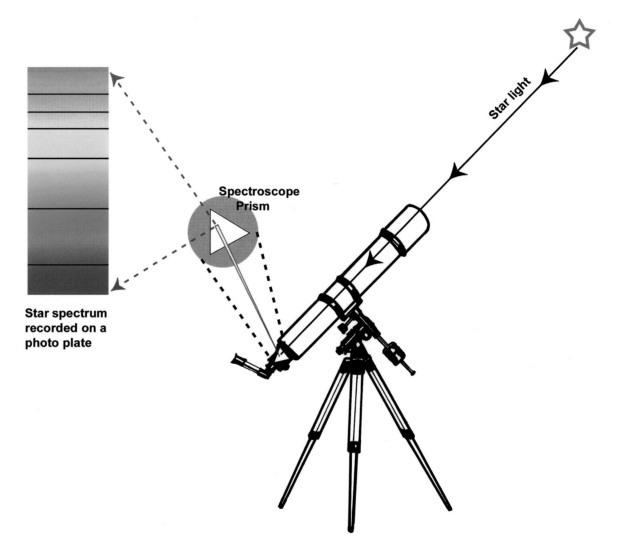

Star spectrum recorded on a photo plate

Spectroscope Prism

Star light

Inside a spectroscope is a prism that splits and separates starlight into a wide rainbow pattern of colors with black lines between them. This is the star's spectrum, its chemical fingerprint that reveals precisely what elements make up the star.

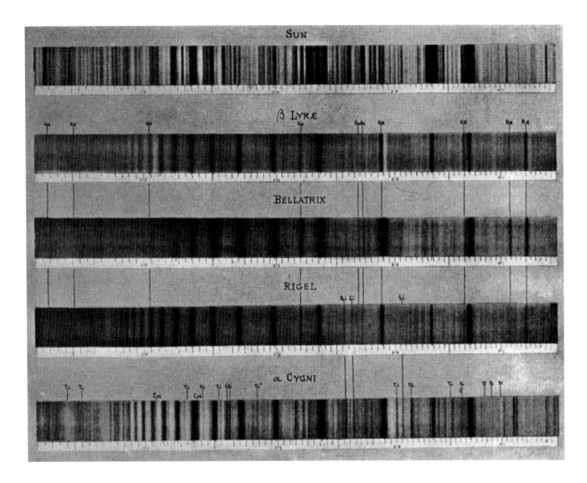

SUN

β LYRÆ

BELLATRIX

RIGEL

α CYGNI

This is one of William and Lady Huggins's spectrographs of different stars' light, including our sun for comparison.

ness in order to see the spectra created. He designed a new kind of spectroscope that could be swapped out with the eyepiece of his telescope. "Then it was that an astronomical observatory began, for the first time, to take on the appearance of a laboratory," Huggins wrote. "Primary batteries, giving forth noxious gases, were arranged outside one of the windows; a large induction coil stood mounted on a stand on wheels so as to follow the positions of the eye-end of the telescope, together with a battery of several [capacitor] jars; shelves with Bunsen burners, vacuum tubes, and bottles of chemicals . . . lined its walls." It was astronomy with the tools of chemistry and physics. **Astrophysics** was born.

By 1864 William Huggins had a working spectral atlas of the known chemical elements. Like a catalog of fingerprints, he could now identify the chemical makeup of what he observed through the telescope. The stars were made up of the very same elements that are here on Earth!

Huggins immediately put his spectroscope to use making his greatest discovery. It was the evening of August 29, 1864. William

now. Putting spectroscopy to work in astronomy gave him a new way to study the stars. By looking at the lines of starlight spectra he could find out what elements were contained in stars of all sorts. All he needed to do was figure out how to hook up a spectroscope to his telescope.

It was easier said than done. Starlight is faint, so Huggins had to work in near dark-

Huggins pointed his telescope for the first time toward a star in the constellation Draco. "I put my eye to the spectroscope," Huggins wrote of his big night. "Was I not about to look into a secret place of creation?" The drama was rooted in the then-controversial nature of nebulae.

Something that's "nebulous" is cloudy or unclear. So when the Herschels and other early astronomers focused their telescopes on a cloudlike object, they called it a **nebula**. (The Herschels charted thousands of them.)

As telescopes got better and zoomed in on these so-called nebulae, some turned out to be masses of stars. Andromeda and Pleiades may look like fuzzy clouds from your backyard. An up-close look, however, shows that they are made up of many individual stars. Hadn't Galileo himself discovered this about the Milky Way? The argument in Huggins's day was whether or not all nebulae were out-of-focus groups of stars. Or were some nebulae actually something else entirely? Something made of a mysterious luminous matter?

As Huggins looked at the nebula in Draco through his spectroscope, he knew that a group of stars would show the rainbow-like spectra similar to sunlight. But this is not what he saw. "No such spectrum as I expected! A single bright line only!" he wrote. Huggins wondered if his instruments were working right. "The thought was scarcely more than momentary; then the true interpretation flashed upon me. . . . The light of the nebula was monochromatic." A single-colored light, the spectral line of a glowing gas unlike any he'd yet seen. "The riddle of

Left: Lady Huggins was an accomplished astronomer as well.

Below: The nebula that Huggins studied, now often called the Cat's Eye Nebula. *NASA, ESA, HEIC, and the Hubble Heritage Team (STScI/AURA)*

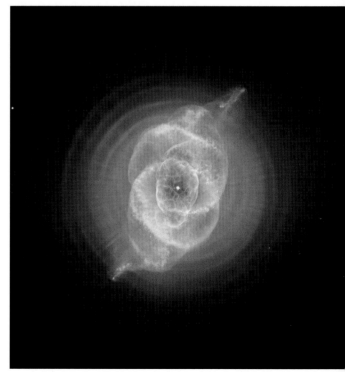

Sir William Huggins (1824–1910)

William Huggins was an amateur astronomer with little formal education. The well-off Englishman built a private observatory at Tulse Hill, London, and taught himself how to use it. After learning about the discoveries in light, or spectrum, analysis he set to work applying them to astronomy.

Huggins designed a spectroscope for his telescope and began making observations in 1863. He showed that stars are made of the same chemical elements as the Earth and Sun. Then he collected spectra from nebulae, proving their gaseous nature. Comets were next to be studied by him. Huggins discovered carbon-based chemicals, called hydrocarbons, in comets.

In 1875 Huggins married Margaret Lindsay (1848–1915), a woman with a shared interest in astronomy. The couple worked as a team from then on, publishing many research papers. William Huggins was knighted in 1897.

the nebulae was solved. The answer, which had come to us in the light itself, read: Not an aggregation of stars, but a luminous gas."

William Huggins had discovered true nebula, glowing clouds of gases and dust. Some nebulae give birth to stars, perhaps making them "secret places of creation," as Huggins suggested.

William Huggins later married a woman interested in astronomy. Together William and Margaret Huggins went on to collect and catalog the patterns of light coming from many stars. They were explorers, finding and describing stars as never before seen.

HUMAN COMPUTERS

Humans have long known that stars come in colors. Even with the naked eye, the star Sirius looks blue-white, while Arcturus looks reddish. With the invention of the spectroscope, astronomers discovered that those colors come from the gases in the stars.

But knowing what creates the color doesn't tell us the reason for the differences. Why are the spectra of some stars one color and not another? And what does it tell us about that star? Astronomers needed more information to find out exactly what stars were and how they came to be. An American named Edward Pickering was working on just that as the 19th century came to an end.

As the director of the Harvard College Observatory in Massachusetts, Pickering was trying to put it all together. His job was to create a catalog of stars, classifying hundreds of thousands of them by their gases. It would take decades in a time when horses powered taxis and electricity was a novelty. At night, Pickering's astronomers photographed starscapes through telescopes armed with spectroscopes. The spectra of hundreds of stars showed up on each glass plate's black-and-white photo. The job of analyzing, sorting, and categorizing the spectra was done by a team of women, nicknamed "computers." Annie Jump Cannon was among them.

As a young girl in Delaware, Cannon's mother taught her eldest daughter the

constellations and how to read star charts.
When night skies over the Cannon household were clear, Annie Jump Cannon and her
mother would make their way onto the roof.
Outside on top of the large, three-story home
was a great place to stargaze.

Annie Cannon never lost her love of
stargazing. She went on to study physics
at Wellesley College, but opportunities for
women in science were scarce in the 1890s,
when Cannon graduated. Cannon returned
home, took up photography, traveled, and
grew restless. "I am sometimes very dissatisfied with my life here. I do want to accomplish
something, so badly," she wrote in her journal.

After her mother died suddenly, 30-year-
old Cannon decided to make a change.
She went back to Wellesley College in 1894
to work as a teaching assistant and study
astronomy. One of her professors was Edward
Pickering, the astronomer in charge of the
star spectra catalog project. In 1896 he hired
Cannon as one of his computers. Helping
to record, classify, and catalog stars by their
light became Cannon's life's work.

Pickering supported the right of women
to vote (which didn't happen until 1920) and

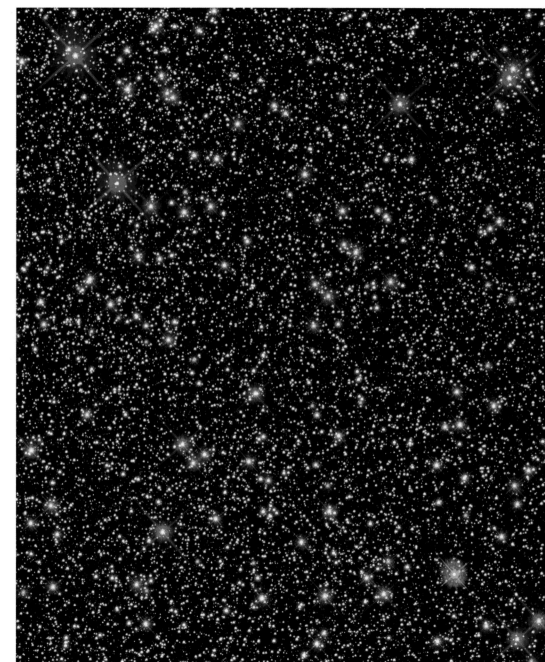

This *Hubble*
Space Telescope
image shows
the many colors
of stars. *NASA*

Harvard Observatory's computer room.

and information into a notebook. The fingerprint-like dark lines of the spectra identified the star's type, color, and temperature.

Cannon was able to relay all the needed information about a star faster than any other computer. She could classify multiple stars per minute, and some 50,000 to 60,000 stars a year. Annie Jump Cannon became known as "the census-taker of the stars."

"They aren't just streaks to me," Cannon once said about the lines of the starlight spectra. "Each new spectrum is the gateway to a wonderful new world. It is almost as if the distant stars had really acquired speech and were able to tell of their constitution and physical condition."

Eventually classifying some quarter of a million stars, Cannon's work and those of the other female computers filled nine volumes of the *Henry Draper Catalogue*. The catalog of stars and starlight was named for the wealthy astronomer Henry Draper, whose heirs funded the project.

When Annie Jump Cannon started working at the Harvard Observatory, Pickering was using a simple lettering system from A to Q to classify stars. But as the women

he also knew a bargain when he saw one. To build a database of stars he needed lots of smart, careful, detailed workers. The women earned 50 cents an hour, so Pickering could hire three or four educated women for the price of one man.

STARRY CENSUS TAKER

The computer room at the Harvard College Observatory looked more like an old-fashioned library. Tall bookshelves,

printed wallpaper, and framed pictures surrounded the wooden tables, which were covered in papers and books. Women with hair pulled into buns and wearing long dresses with high collars sat erect in straight-backed chairs. The female computers held magnifying glasses and looked at glass plates propped up on viewing stands lit by mirrors. They called out facts about each star's spectrum on the photo plate to a "recorder," an assistant who wrote down the numbers

Annie Jump Cannon (1863–1941)

Annie Jump Cannon was born during the Civil War, the oldest daughter of a Delaware state senator. Encouraged by her parents to get the best education possible, Cannon attended a once-boys-only school, and then went on to the only women's college to offer physics classes.

Cannon lost much of her hearing while at college. A bad case of scarlet fever led to a damaging ear infection. She wore a hearing aid the rest of her life. However, her disability didn't stop Cannon from studying physics and astronomy, as she'd planned.

As was expected in those days, Cannon returned to her parents' home after graduating. For nearly a decade she tried to amuse herself with photography and music. It was not until her mother passed away that Cannon returned to college to take up astronomy again.

Cannon worked at Harvard classifying stars for the rest of her life. She also discovered some 300 variable stars and five **novae**—stars that flare in brightness from an explosion and then fade. In 1925, Cannon was the first woman to receive an honorary doctorate from the University of Oxford in England, and she was the first woman to become an officer in the American Astronomical Society.

analyzed more and more starlight spectra, the labeling system worked less and less well. Groups of letters were first combined to improve the categories. Then some were later abandoned and everything reshuffled—making a confusing mess. Cannon understood that a classification system that was hard to understand wasn't useful. She decided that

star temperature was something researchers could agree on and use to classify stars. After all, they'd been labeling the hottest stars with the letter O for years. It made sense to her to organize all stars by their temperature—from hottest to coolest.

Because of all the shuffling that had happened along the way, the seven categories

ended up being: O, B, A, F, G, K, and M. Cannon made up the now-famous mnemonic device to help others remember the system: **Oh, Be A Fine Girl. Kiss Me**. It's helped generations of astronomers remember that O stars are hot and M stars are not. Cannon's spectral-type classification system is still used today, but made more precise by

Discoveries Closer to Home

The 18th and 19th centuries were a time of exploration within our own solar system, too. In fact, the hundred years between 1780 and 1880 saw the known solar system more than triple in size!

A famous comet passed though our solar system in 1758. English scientist Edmund Halley studied past observations and in 1705 predicted a comet would appear in 53 years. When it did, right on schedule, comet Halley was appropriately named.

William Herschel's discovery of Uranus through his telescope in 1781 was a huge deal. The five planets known at the time—Mercury, Venus, Mars, Jupiter, and Saturn—had been part of human history for millennia. All were visible with the naked eye and had been tracked and observed by the earliest humans. Uranus is about 1.78 billion miles (2.87 billion km) from the Sun. That's a bit more than twice Saturn's distance, so Herschel's discovery doubled the size of the known solar system.

Uranus's discovery got people wondering if perhaps other planets were out there circling the Sun. This led to Johann Galle finding Neptune, the eighth planet, in 1846. Neptune added another chunk of landscape to the solar system. The planet is so far from the Sun that it takes nearly 165 Earth years to complete one orbit.

Comet Halley streaking in front of the Milky Way in 1986. *NASA*

adding the numbers 0 through 9. Our sun is a G2 star, for example, which is hotter than a G3 star.

Being able to sort and classify stars was an important step for astronomers. As Annie Jump Cannon wrote in 1915, "The results will help to unravel some of the mysteries of the great universe, visible to us, in the depths above. They will provide material for investigation of those distant suns of which we know nothing except as revealed by the rays of light, travelling for years with great velocity through space, to be made at last to tell their magical story on our photographic plates."

Astronomers now had a database with which to study the stars. What patterns would emerge, and what discoveries would the stars reveal next?

DANISH DREAMER

Not all discoveries about the stars happen in the middle of the night while peering through a telescope. Astronomer Ejnar Hertzsprung did most of his work sitting at a desk.

Hertzsprung was from Copenhagen, Denmark. His father had studied astronomy, passing his interest in the stars onto his son. He covered one of their living-room windows with a star chart. The chart's stars shone from sunlight coming through pinholes sized to match each star's magnitude. As a small boy, Ejnar would lie on the floor gazing at the star chart for hours.

Ejnar also inherited his father's doubts about stargazing. The elder Hertzsprung had been unable to earn a living with astronomy, and so his son chose chemistry as a career. Ejnar Hertzsprung became an expert in the chemicals and processes used in photography at the time.

When Hertzsprung decided to take up astronomy full-time in 1901, it was on his own, not at a university or observatory full of telescopes and expensive equipment. But he had a desk and lots of information that needed studying.

The catalogs of starlight types, star motions, positions, and estimated distances were piling up by the turn of the century. The data showed that stars were not all alike. Stars were individuals with different temperatures, brightnesses, and colors. But what did all this information describing

Ejnar Hertzsprung looking at spectrograph plates around 1930.

Dorritt Hoffleit, Yale University Observatory, courtesy AIP Emilio Segre Visual Archives

and categorizing so many stars really mean? Were there patterns or connections among their properties? This was the next step for star-studying scientists like Hertzsprung. "If one works hard," he was known to say, "one always finds something and sometimes something important." And find something important he did.

A MEANINGFUL RELATIONSHIP

Hertzsprung started to find patterns in the data. He discovered that the color of a star tells you a lot—including its temperature, brightness, and size. Blue-white O stars are brighter, hotter, and larger than B stars. This holds true down through A, F, G, and K stars to the cool, small, red, fainter M stars. A star's color and brightness are related.

Around the same time, American astronomer Henry Norris Russell realized the same thing. In 1913 he published a graph that plotted the color of stars versus their brightness—**spectral type** versus **luminosity**. Most stars in the graph tended to line up along a diagonal band. The brightness of a star decreased with its temperature. The findings came to be called the **Hertzsprung-Russell Diagram**, though Hertzsprung didn't like the name. "Why not call it the color-magnitude diagram?" he asked. "Then we would know what it is about."

The Hertzsprung-Russell (H-R) Diagram is still an important tool for astronomers today. The H-R diagram shows how a star's luminosity, spectral type, color, and temperature are related. Knowing that our sun is a G star tells you it is yellow, has a medium brightness, and burns at about 6,000° C.

Thousands of stars fall into three basic groups on the diagram. **Main sequence stars** make up the largest group, which includes our sun. Main sequence stars follow the "brighter is hotter" rule, creating the diagonal band Hertzsprung saw. Rare **red giants**, such as the star Betelgeuse, are bright but cool. The third group is **white dwarfs**, stars that are hot but dim.

Diagrams are helpful tools. Sometimes looking at information on a graph or chart makes finding patterns easier. What's most important often pops out. This is what happened with the H-R diagram. Looking at it made astronomers wonder whether the different colors and temperatures of stars were

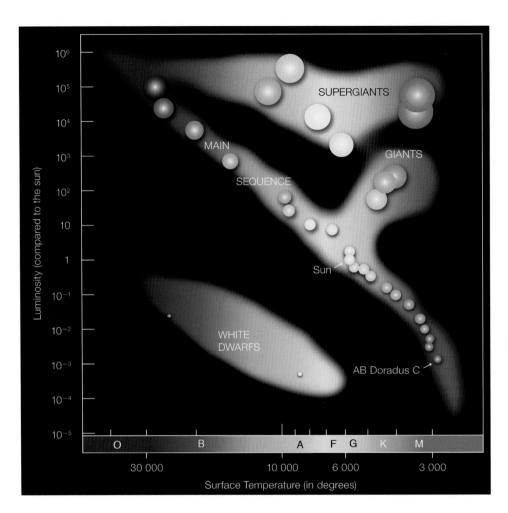

The Hertzsprung-Russell Diagram plots luminosity (brightness) against spectral class (temperature).
ESO

different stages of the same process. Did stars burn brightly as blue stars, then grow fainter with time, becoming dim, red stars?

It didn't turn out to be quite that simple. In the early 1900s, no one understood what fueled stars. The fact that deep inside a star is a **nuclear fusion** reactor of hydrogen changing into helium wasn't yet discovered. But the idea that stars go through stages—that they grow, age, evolve, and change over eons—was right. The stars that populate the universe live lives. Stars are born, live, and die.

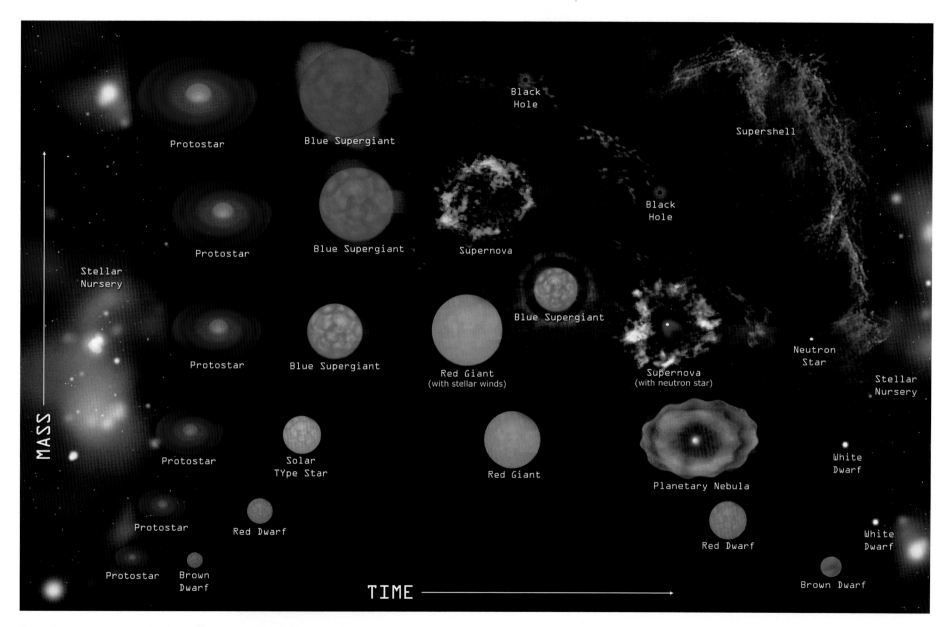

A star's mass determines the life it lives. *NASA/CXC/M.Weiss*

Albert Einstein at work in the
Swiss Patent Office in 1904.

NASA/courtesy of nasaimages.org

4 1900–1940: Space-Time Tricks, Island Universes, and the Biggest Bang

Hermann Einstein felt sorry for his son, Albert. The five-year-old boy had been sick in bed for days. So Father brought home a gift to amuse little Albert. It was a pocket compass. The simple instrument fascinated the boy. The way the compass needle always pointed the same way amazed Albert. No matter how he moved it, the compass kept pointing north! What invisible force was at work? Albert wondered. "I can still remember . . . that this experience made a deep and lasting impression on me," remembered Albert Einstein. "Something deeply hidden had to be behind things." And to Einstein, something hidden is something begging to be discovered.

This deep curiosity was what made Einstein one of the greatest scientists of all time. Science, for Einstein, was a way to understand the mysteries and wonders of the natural world. He wasn't like most scientists, who studied one topic within a single subject, such as chemistry or biology. Einstein wanted to answer fundamental science questions, such as: What is light? What is gravity? What is time? What is energy? Laboratory experiments couldn't really answer them. Einstein instead used his mind to work them out. Imagination and mathmatics were the tools of his "thought experiments." And his early laboratory was a patent office, where he worked as a clerk.

DEEPLY HIDDEN, UNSEEN FORCES

Around the turn of the 20th century, new inventions sprouted like mushrooms—light bulbs, telephones, airplanes, radios, electric motors, and more. Factories, cities, and citizens welcomed lit-up living rooms and phone calls from friends. But the discovery that enabled many of these inventions—**electromagnetism**—created a pile of questions that scientists couldn't answer.

The behavior of electricity and magnets poked holes in the ideas of Isaac Newton that had guided science for nearly 300 years. Newton's law of gravity said that objects in the universe are attracted to each other. The strength of that attraction depends on the size, or mass, of those objects and the distance between them. The Sun's gravity tugs more on Earth than Earth pulls on the moon because the Sun is much more massive. Likewise, the Sun's gravity pulls more on Venus than it does on Pluto because Pluto is farther away.

Newton's law of gravity accurately described the way the planets orbit the Sun and how objects fall to the earth. But while Newton could explain what gravity did, he didn't know what caused it. He described gravity as an invisible, mysterious force of attraction. And that was good enough, since Newton's laws of gravity and motion worked perfectly well in the everyday world.

The discovery of electromagnetism changed that. Electricity, magnetism, and light are different than planets and falling apples. They don't follow the rules of Newton's universe, where the strength of forces depends on distance and mass. Electricity and magnetism are forces that instead depend on fields. A magnetic field, for example, is an active area around a magnet. Likewise, an electrically charged object affects the space around it. Electromagnetism, including light of all kinds, travels in waves that affects the space around it.

Trying to understand how the forces of electromagnetic fields and those of gravity are different—and related—was the Big Question around the turn of the last century. As a young college student in Zurich, Switzerland, Albert Einstein certainly pondered it.

COSMIC SPEED LIMITS

The universe Isaac Newton described was always the same everywhere. An hour on Mount Everest is the same amount of time as on a Martian mountain, too. A 12-inch ruler on a desk in Kansas is the same length as one on a spaceship speeding past Pluto. No one had had a problem with Newton's permanent, unchanging universe of space and time for hundreds of years.

Realizing that Newton's laws couldn't explain how electromagnetism worked was quite a shock to scientists—including Einstein. "It was as if the ground had been pulled out from under one, with no firm foundation to be seen anywhere," he said. But it also opened a new door to understanding—one that Albert Einstein walked right through.

Many of Einstein's discoveries come from his famous equation: $E = mc^2$; where E is energy, m is mass, and c is the speed of light. What does it mean? First, that mass and energy can be changed into each other and so are just different forms of the same thing. An object's mass is also a measure of how much energy it holds, Einstein said. Second, because the speed of light is such a big number, a tiny bit of mass can equal a lot of energy, according to the equation.

The idea that a small amount of mass can produce a huge amount of energy is a big deal, especially for astronomers. It explains why stars burn and glow for millions of years. The amount (or mass) of hydrogen in a star makes a whole lot of energy when nuclear fusion changes it to energy. Each century, our own sun only uses up a tiny fraction—about 6.6 parts in a trillion—of its hydrogen to light and heat our entire solar system. Einstein's equation unites energy, matter, and light—and finally explains what fuels the stars!

$E = mc^2$ also explains why nothing can go faster than the speed of light. Einstein's famous equation says that the faster something moves, the more massive it gets. The more massive (m) an object becomes, the more pushing power (E) it needs to keep up its speed. For an object to be pushed with enough energy to travel 186,000 miles per second (c), its mass must become infinite. That's not possible, nor is the infinite amount of energy that would be needed to move infinite mass possible. Traveling faster than the speed of light is impossible. The cosmos has a speed limit.

SQUISHY SPACE-TIME

Einstein also figured out that the speed of light is always the same. And if light speed can't change, then it must be other factors that do change—such as time.

Try your own thought experiment: A passenger in a subway train car traveling 1 meter per second walks to the door nearest the

A sculpture of Einstein's famous equation in front of Old Museum in Berlin, Germany.

Anders Thirsgaard Rasmussen

front of the train. She then turns around and aims a laser pointer at a mirror at the far end of the train car. The light travels the 2 meters to the mirror (and then bounces back to the passenger). You're standing on the platform and see into the passing subway car as the passenger flashes the laser light. Do you see the light travel 2 meters to the mirror, like the passenger did? Nope, the light traveled a shorter distance for you because the mirror in the moving subway car moved closer to the point at which the laser was fired.

You and the passenger disagree on the distance the light traveled, but not on the speed of light (since it never changes). Speed is distance divided by time—meters divided by seconds in this case. The difference in distance you and the passenger observed the light travel is really a difference in how much time passed. This is Einstein's theory of **relativity**. Time is not absolute; it is relative. Both you and the passengers have your own different measure of time.

"The distinction between the past, present, and future is only a stubbornly persistent illusion," said Einstein. Maybe, but the fact that time isn't the same for everyone everywhere is hard to grasp. It's not something you notice in the ordinary world. It's often counterintuitive, too, going against common sense. But people during Copernicus's day said the same thing about a spinning Earth moving around the Sun. We don't feel all that motion, so it also seems unreal. But it is real—just relative.

Newton's laws of motion hold up for most everyday situations, and his equations were good enough to send men to the moon. But relativity is needed to understand what's ordinary out in the cosmos. Astronomers study massive objects over long distances. Light from these objects can take millions of years to travel to Earth. An astronomer might see one star exploding and another one being eclipsed on the same night. But because of the stars' differing distances from Earth, the two events may have happened millions of years apart in time.

In fact, not only is time relative, so is space itself. Einstein called it **space-time**. Time is a fourth dimension, inseparable from space. As Einstein said, "The only reason for time is so that everything doesn't happen at once." Exactly *where* something is depends on *when*. There is no *here* separate from *now*. There is only here-and-now. Space and time. That's space-time.

Many think of space-time as a constantly changing medium or framework. Space-time can be bent and warped, dented and indented by massive objects, said Einstein. This is what gravity is: a curve in space-time.

Einstein published his theory of **general relativity** in 1915. It redefined gravity, proposing that mass warps both time and space. Think about it this way: Space-time is like a stretchy fabric or squishy sofa cushion. Heavy things with lots of mass are like bowling balls on that cushion. Massive objects bend the fabric of space-time and sink into holes with sloping walls. Nearby matter flows down these slopes in space-time. This is what gravity is. It is the force that keeps planets in orbit around the Sun.

Gravity doesn't pull an apple off a tree. The curvature of space-time creates gravity. Space and time in Einstein's universe are not rigid and fixed, but are flexible, pushable, and changeable by matter. Gravity feels strongest where space-time is most curved, and it vanishes where space-time is uncurved. Matter affects how space-time curves, and curved space-time affects how matter moves. As Einstein summed up, "Time and space and gravitation have no separate existence from matter."

PUTTING RELATIVITY TO THE TEST

Thought experiments are interesting, but what about proof? How could Einstein convince physicists that gravity comes from

Warp Some T-Shirt Space-Time

activity

Einstein redefined gravity in 1916 with his theory of general relativity. Space isn't endless emptiness, it's a fabric that grips matter and is warped by it, too. This space-time fabric is bent and twisted by objects with mass, such as stars. Deforming space-time alters the shape of space, as well as the passage of time. You can model Einstein's universe yourself, using a T-shirt.

YOU'LL NEED

⇒ Old T-shirt

⇒ Dish tub, organizer basket, boot box, etc.

⇒ Marbles or small balls

⇒ Round stone or ball of clay

1. Stretch a T-shirt over a tub, basket, or box so that the fabric is taut. You may need to try a smaller T-shirt or larger tub or bin to get the fabric taut enough. (If the shirt is a rag, you can cut it and tape it to the bin or box to make it fit tightly.) The taut T-shirt represents space-time. Its shape represents gravity.

2. Roll some of the marbles across space-time. Watch how they curve. The marbles aren't pulled by gravity, they are simply following the curve in space-time caused by their own mass.

3. Set a stone or clay ball in the center of your space-time fabric. This massive object represents a sun.

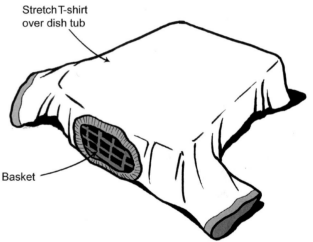

Stretch T-shirt over dish tub

Basket

Clay ball

Marbles

4. Repeat step 2, observing how the sun's mass deforms space-time and affects the planetary marbles' paths.

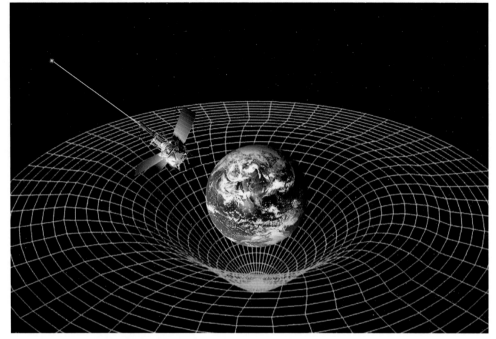

Gravity Probe B orbited Earth in 2004–05 in a successful test of Einstein's theory of general relativity. Four ultraprecise gyroscopes measured the warping of space and time around Earth. *NASA*

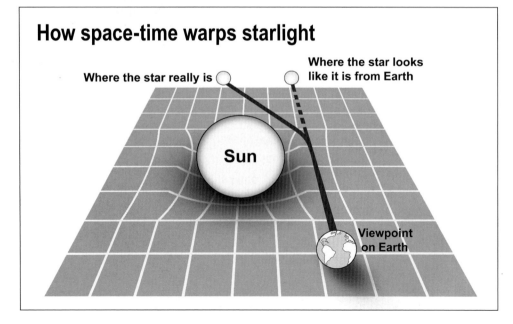

How space-time warps starlight

Where the star really is

Where the star looks like it is from Earth

Sun

Viewpoint on Earth

changes in space-time? He needed an experiment, a test to prove it to the world. What is something with enough gravity to bend space-time that is near enough to Earth to photograph? wondered Einstein.

The Sun! Our star holds 99 percent of the solar system's mass, after all. It makes a big enough dent in space-time to bend even starlight going around it. But the Sun is also very bright, making it impossible to see starlight near it. Yet Einstein realized that during a daytime solar eclipse the Sun was visible but darkened. An astronomer could take a photograph showing the position of a star behind the Sun during an eclipse. By comparing the star's position to a nighttime photo of the same star, the bending path of starlight should show up. The light from the star will be pulled inward by the Sun's gravity, making the star look like it is farther out.

As straightforward as it sounds, the test wasn't easy to accomplish. Einstein wasn't an astronomer. He tried for years to get someone with the right kind of telescope and camera to go to a place where a full eclipse was happening. World War I got in the way, too. A German astronomer on a 1914 eclipse expedition for Einstein to the Russian Crimea ended up a prisoner of war.

Another chance came on May 29, 1919. A total eclipse of the Sun was going to be observable over parts of South America and Africa. With the war over and Britain its victor, Sir Arthur Eddington was able to get the funding such an expedition required. The British astronomer was a big fan of Einstein and his theory of relativity. Loaded with equipment, Eddington set sail for the Príncipe Island, off Africa's western coast.

The morning of May 29, 1919, began with a violent tropical rainstorm. Weather had ruined earlier attempts to observe eclipses. Would it doom this one, too? By the time the clouds cleared, the Sun was already starting to become shadowed by the moon. Watching darkness creep over the Sun is quite an experience. Eddington and his crew weren't there as eclipse tourists, however. "We have no time to snatch a glance at it," he wrote. The total eclipse, when the sky is darkest, would only last 302 seconds. Five minutes was all the time they had to photograph it, using glass plates that had to be changed out with each shot. "We are conscious only

of the weird half-light of the landscape and the hush of nature, broken by the calls of the observers."

Eddington got 16 photographs that day, only a few of which were free of star-blotting clouds. But it was enough. In the photos, streams of starlight bent around the darkened Sun. The difference was as Einstein predicted. Relativity could be measured and seen. It was real.

Newspapers ran headlines saying NEWTONIAN IDEAS OVERTHROWN, MEN

Left: One of the photographs of the solar eclipse of May 29, 1919, used to confirm that space-time bends starlight toward the Sun.

Above: The British astronomer who helped Einstein prove relativity by photographing the 1919 eclipse, Sir Arthur Stanley Eddington.

Library of Congress, Prints and Photographs Division

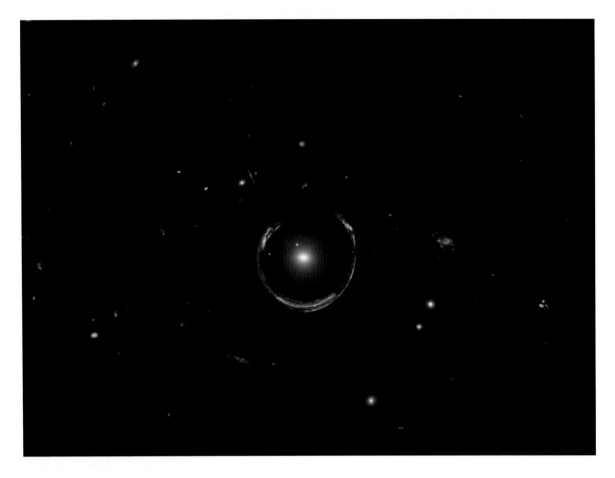

This blue halo is a distant galaxy warped by the light-bending gravity of the center red galaxy into an illusion called an Einstein Ring.
ESA/Hubble & NASA

precise enough to show the difference in time between sea level and on mountaintops, where gravity is less strong and space-time less bent. They can also measure the slowing effect of going really fast. The watch on the wrist of a pilot in a super-fast jet ticks more slowly than yours does.

Albert Einstein's theory of general relativity led to all sorts of astronomical discoveries. One that Einstein himself didn't particularly like was that the universe was unstable. Einstein's own theory of gravity described a universe where stars and everything else would eventually clump together. Einstein, like most astronomers at the time, believed in a stable universe, not a collapsing one. To "fix" this problem, Einstein decided there must be some as-yet-unknown force that pushes back against the collapsing universe, keeping it stable. He called this the cosmological constant and added it to his equations in 1917.

Years later, Einstein would call his cosmological constant "the biggest blunder of my life." What changed his mind? Proof that the universe is not only unstable, but also expanding. That discovery came from a young astronomer and a very big telescope.

of Science More or Less Agog Over Results of Eclipse Observations, and Stars Not Where They Seemed.

FAME AND CHANGE

Albert Einstein became famous around the world. Two years later he won the Nobel Prize in Physics. Einstein's theories have passed other tests since then. Clocks are now

A Toy with No Equal activity

Albert Einstein was given a simple toy for his 76th birthday that demonstrates the equivalence of gravity and acceleration, an important part of understanding general relativity. Make one yourself and see if it helps explain Einstein's ideas.

YOU'LL NEED

➡ Cup-a-soup or similarly sized wide Styrofoam or plastic cup

➡ Nail or sharp pen

➡ Long 6–8 inch (15–20 cm) rubber band

➡ Scissors

➡ 2 small but heavy balls

➡ Heavy tape or glue

➡ Paper clip

➡ 6 pennies

1. Turn the cup upside down and push a nail or sharp pen into the center of its bottom. Wiggle out the nail so you're left with a hole.

2. Cut the rubber band open. Tape or glue one ball onto each end.

3. Bend a paper clip so that it becomes a small hook. Stick the hook end through the hole in the bottom of the cup. Use it to grab on to the middle of the rubber band and pull it just through the hole.

4. Make sure the balls hang evenly over the sides of the cup, stretching the rubber bands somewhat, and that the paper clip is holding the middle of the rubber band. Rebend the paper clip so it lies flat on the bottom of the cup and tape or glue it down.

5. Place the pennies on the bottom of the cup and tape or glue them down, too. This gives the cup more weight.

6. Here's the question: How do you get the balls into the cup by using what you know about the equivalence between gravity and acceleration? Try it out! Hold the cup out in front of you with your arms raised and the balls hanging outside the cup. Let go of the cup, letting it fall a couple of feet before catching it. When you drop the cup, it goes into free fall, accelerating downward. The directions of the force of gravity and the cup's acceleration are opposite, but the forces are equal, so they cancel each other out. Because there is no gravitational force stretching the rubber bands, they pull the balls into the cup *as it falls*. Puzzle solved!

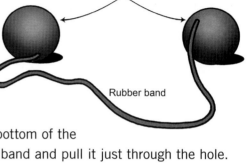

Small heavy ball

Rubber band

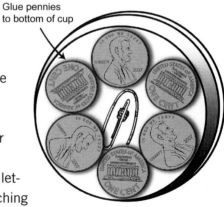

Glue pennies to bottom of cup

Foam cup

Albert Einstein (1879–1955)

Albert Einstein was born in Germany. His family claims he was slow to learn to speak but was always a curious child who loved to play violin. He later credited his development of the theory of relativity to being a late bloomer. Einstein said, "The ordinary adult never gives a thought to space-time problems. . . . I, on the contrary, developed so slowly that I did not begin to wonder about space and time until I was an adult. I then delved more deeply into the problem than any other adult or child would have done."

Young Albert didn't thrive in the strict German schools of the day, and teachers criticized his daydreaming during class. As a teenager he moved to Italy with his family and finished high school in Switzerland, where he also went to college. Einstein also failed to impress his university professors. He was known to skip classes, flirt with girls, and study what he wanted to instead of what was assigned.

By 1901 Albert Einstein had become a Swiss citizen. He also found himself a college graduate unable to get a job, so he was unable to marry and support his fiancée. A friend finally helped him get a clerk job in Bern at a patent office. It was while working there from 1902 to 1909 that Einstein made many of his important discoveries, including $E = mc^2$. The papers he wrote about relativity, the existence of atoms, and the nature of light made him a respected physicist.

From then on he held positions at universities—first in Switzerland, then Germany, and later in the United States. He moved to the United States after the Nazi Party took over Germany in 1933. As a Jewish person, the country of his birth was no longer safe. He became an American citizen in 1940.

After explaining the nature of gravity in his theory of general relativity, Einstein worked on an even bigger idea. It was a theory that would include all electric, magnetic, and gravitational forces. Einstein worked on this unified field theory for the rest of his life, without success. No one has yet developed a unified field theory.

These stamps from Cuba commemorate Einstein's 1930 visit to the Caribbean country.

Sweet, Twisted Space-Time

activity

Einstein described gravity as curved space-time in 1916. Other physicists soon added on to his theory, predicting that masses could deform space-time in more than one way. A massive object, such as a planet, not only curves the shape of space-time around it. If it is spinning, it will also twist space-time near it. This twisting of space-time is called frame-dragging, since a spinning planet drags the local frame of reference around itself.

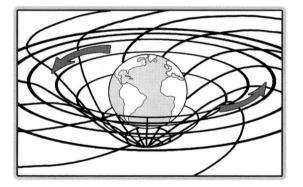

Here's a simple and sweet way to see how frame-dragging works.

YOU'LL NEED

➡ Honey

➡ Small bowl or dish

➡ Small ball

➡ Liquid food coloring

1. Pour 1 inch (2.5 cm) or so of honey into a bowl. The honey is space-time.

2. Set a small ball in the center of the bowl. It represents Earth or another spinning space object.

3. Squeeze a drop of food coloring into the honey near the ball.

4. Now use your fingers to quickly spin the ball. Observe how the honey and food coloring turns with it. Where is space-time (honey) being pulled around more, near or far from Earth (ball)? As Earth spins, it drags local space-time around with it, especially closer to the planet.

Honey

Food coloring

Left: Workers haul the 100-inch mirror for the Hooker Telescope up Mount Wilson in 1917.

Right: Mount Wilson Observatory's Hooker Telescope was the largest in the world when it was built in the 1910s.

WAR BEFORE WORK

A job working on the biggest telescope in the world doesn't come around every day. But 27-year-old Edwin Powell Hubble wouldn't take the offer—at least not right away. Hubble gave his answer in a telegram, saying: "Regret cannot accept your invitation to join the Mount Wilson staff. Joined the Army instead. Am off to war." It was 1917, and the young astronomer went to fight in Europe. Mount Wilson Observatory would have to

wait until World War I ended before it got Edwin Hubble.

Mount Wilson Observatory sits atop Mount Wilson, a 5,715-foot (1,742 m) peak in the San Gabriel Mountains near Pasadena, California. In 1919, after the war was over, Edwin Hubble finally showed up for work at the observatory. In those days it was a long, bumpy truck ride to the top. The narrow road zigzagged up to the collection of buildings and domes that made up Mount Wilson Observatory.

The ride was worth the view. On a clear day, Edwin Hubble could see Los Angeles to the south and the Pacific Ocean to the west. It was a perfect spot to study the heavens—especially with the new Hooker Telescope. The giant telescope had taken more than a decade to build. Its mirror was 100 inches (250 cm) across, the biggest in the world. It had taken a truck with four motors to haul the huge mirror up the mountain, with a mule team dragging it up the steepest sections. Workers installed the mirror onto a steel frame inside a dome. The frame rested on ball bearings floating in a tank filled with mercury. This allowed astronomers to pivot the 100-ton telescope into position by hand.

The Hooker 100-inch telescope at Mount Wilson Observatory was the engineering marvel of its day. And it was just the tool needed to decide the question of the day: Where exactly are we in the universe?

ISLAND UNIVERSES

The debate over where we are in the universe came from studying nebulae. Once thought of as heavenly clouds, then discovered to be globs or spirals of stars, nebulae were again confusing astronomers. Where were these objects, exactly?

One leading astronomer, Harlow Shapley (1885–1972), claimed that these nebulae were close to us, within the Milky Way. He believed that the whole universe was just the Milky Way, so of course nebulae are located within it.

Astronomer Heber D. Curtis (1872–1942) disagreed. He argued that the nebulae were too far away to be within the Milky Way. Curtis believed that these cloudy spirals called nebulae were distant, separate "island" universes like our own. This theory meant that the Milky Way wasn't unique—and that we weren't where we thought we were.

Edwin Hubble had studied nebulae in Wisconsin before the war. Once at work at Mount Wilson in California, he got back to it. Using the giant telescope, he photographed large areas of the night sky, looking for nebulae. Hubble was finding all sorts of them—in many shapes, not just spirals.

By 1923, Hubble was concentrating on distances: How far away were these nebulae? Were they within the accepted borders of the Milky Way? If they were beyond them, did it mean they were distant, separate universes? By late summer, Hubble's hunt for evidence of island universes was centered on the Andromeda nebula. It was home to a kind of signpost star, called a **Cepheid**.

Cepheids are variable stars. Each goes back and forth between bright and dim on its own regular schedule, which can be anything from days to months. This time from brightest to dimmest and back to brightest is called a period. In 1912 astronomer Henrietta S. Leavitt (1868–1921), discovered that the length of a Cepheid's period depends on its brightness. The dimmer a Cepheid, the shorter its period. A brighter Cepheid takes longer to go from bright to dim than a less bright one.

This discovery gave astronomers a tool to measure distances across space. If you can see two Cepheids with the same time period but one looks less bright, it must be farther away. It's like looking at distant traffic lights. All of them glow with the same amount of light, but the ones closer to you look brighter.

Edwin Hubble labeled the Cepheid variable star he found in Andromeda "VAR!" on his photo plate. It's now known as the star that changed the universe. *E. Hubble, NASA, ESA, R. Gendler, Z. Levay and the Hubble Heritage Team*

A GALAXY IS BORN

Throughout the summer of 1923, Edwin Hubble photographed and studied the Andromeda nebula. Hubble found a faint Cepheid variable star in the photos. By comparing his photos to older images, he figured out its period, which told him its distance from Earth.

Andromeda was far—very far. In fact, Hubble calculated that it was several times farther from Earth than the edge of the Milky Way. Spiral nebulae, such as Andromeda, were not part of the Milky Way. The nebulae were "extragalactic," or beyond the Milky Way. Hubble's discovery ended the debate. Curtis was right. When Hubble wrote to Shapley to tell him what he'd found, Shapley called it "the letter that destroyed my universe."

Shapley's idea of the universe might have ended, but everyone else's was reborn. "There is just not one universe," Hubble explained to a newspaper reporter. "Countless whole worlds, each of them a mighty universe, are strewn all over the sky. Like the proverbial grains of sand on the beach are the universes, each of them peopled with billions of stars or solar systems."

Our Milky Way isn't the whole universe, it is one of billions of galaxies in a universe stretching for tens of millions of light-years. Nebulae are other Milky Ways—other island universes. Today we call them galaxies. The Andromeda galaxy was the first of many to be recognized. "Science has already taken a census of nearly 10 million galactic systems or individual universes of stars," Hubble told reporters.

Edwin Hubble discovered the existence of galaxies and revealed the universe was a hundred times the size most believed it to be at the time. It made him famous. Headlines read: Ten Million Worlds in the Sky Census and Mount Wilson Observers Now Study Stars on Newly Found Horizons and Light Registered on Photographic Plates Started Million Years Ago.

Hubble kept on studying "extragalactic nebulae," as he called galaxies. He knew that the galaxies in his photographs weren't all

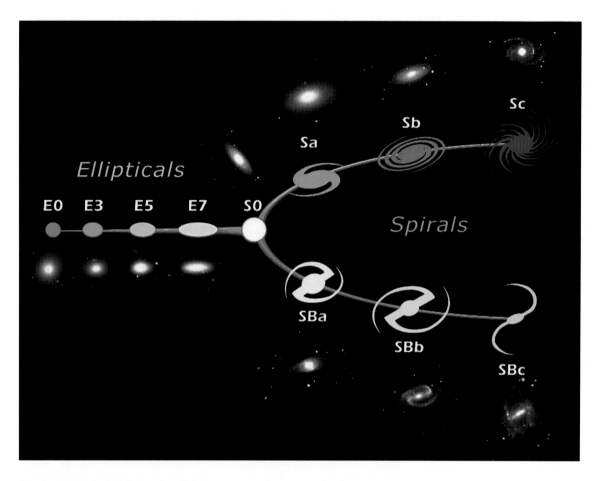

Edwin Hubble's 1926 "tuning fork" diagram of galaxy classification includes elliptical (E) and spiral (S) galaxies. The more oval-shaped an elliptical galaxy is, the higher its number. An E0 is almost round, whereas an E7 is very oval. Spiral galaxies have letters from a to c to rate how compact their arms are. An Sa is tightly wound, an Sc is loosely wound. Spiral galaxies are also divided into normal spirals and barred spirals. The difference between these two groups is the bar of stars that runs through the central bulge in barred spirals. The spiral arms in barred spirals start at the end of the bar, not from the bulge. Barred spirals have a B in their classification. So an SBc is a loosely wound barred spiral galaxy. A galaxy classified as S0 is lenticular, or in between spiral and elliptical. *NASA & ESA E*

Edwin Powell Hubble using the 100-inch telescope at Mount Wilson.

ral galaxies are shaped like giant spinning wheels, flat discs with curved arms coming from the center—like the Milky Way. Elliptical galaxies aren't flat and have no arms, instead being more round or oval-shaped. Irregular galaxies are oddly shaped ones that don't fit into the other two groups.

GALAXIES ON THE RUN

New discoveries have a way of creating new questions. All the time Hubble put into studying and classifying galaxies turned up something startling: the galaxies aren't just far away from us, they're moving farther away all the time. The universe is expanding!

Edwin Hubble measured the speed of galaxies by studying the light coming from them—their spectra. Gathering enough light to make spectrographs of such distant galaxies was a chore, one that mostly fell to Hubble's then assistant Milton L. Humason (1891–1972). "You had to climb onto the 100-inch [telescope] and sit on the iron frame during the long winter nights," said Humason. He had to stay there for hours on freezing nights to make sure the telescope got the image. "The eye-strain, the monotony, the

spirals like Andromeda and our own Milky Way. Galaxies came in other shapes, too. Hubble created a classification system for galaxies that astronomers still use today. It puts galaxies into three main groups based on shape: spiral, elliptical, or irregular. Spi-

constant awareness—it was a test of endurance." But it was worth it. The spectrographs showed something important.

Hubble noticed that the light from distant galaxies was somewhat shifted to the red end of the spectrum. And the farther away a galaxy was, the more its light shifted toward red. The phenomenon is called **redshift**. Starlight from galaxies shifts toward the red end because the light is moving away from us. It's like the changing sound of a fire truck siren. If the siren-screaming truck is coming your way, its pitch sounds higher. Once it passes you and is moving away, the pitch lowers. Red is the low end of light's spectrum, so light zooming away from us shifts red. The galaxies are redshifting because they are moving away from us.

By measuring the amount of redshift, Hubble could measure the speeds of the galaxies. And they were really fast—some moved nearly 25,000 miles (40,000 km) per second. Or as Hubble noted, "around the Earth in a second, out to the moon in 10 seconds, out to the Sun in just over an hour." Hubble admitted to a reporter in 1929 that "it is difficult to believe that the velocities are

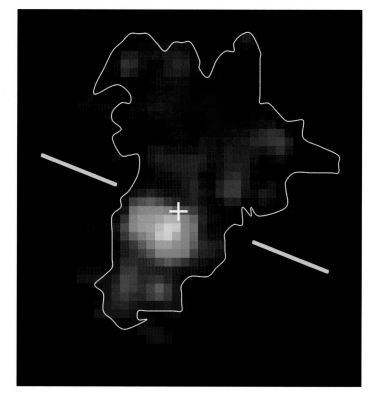

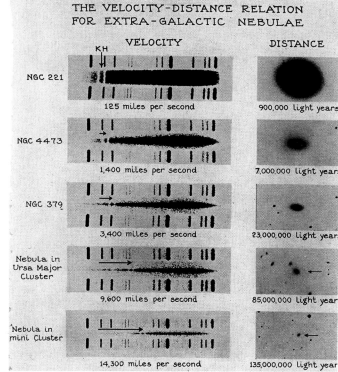

Left: This is a spectrograph of a very large, distant galaxy shaped like our own Milky Way, called BzK-15504. The colors show whether the faraway galaxy's gas is moving away from the Milky Way (red), toward our galaxy (blue), or is stationary (green). *ESO*

Right: This page from Hubble's book *The Realm of the Nebula* compares the distances of galaxies with their speeds, as calculated from redshift. It's proof the universe is expanding.

Expand a Balloon-iverse

In 1929 Edwin Hubble discovered that the universe is expanding. The overall volume of the universe is increasing with this expansion, as are the distances between galaxies. But the galaxies themselves aren't thinning, nor are their stars being diluted by expanding space. The gravitational attraction among the stars within a galaxy is more powerful than the universe's expansion, so the galaxies remain intact and their stars don't drift apart.

YOU'LL NEED

➡ Marker

➡ Small stickers, such as stars or dots

➡ Large, sturdy balloon (such as a punch-ball)

➡ Twist tie or rubber band

➡ Measuring tape

➡ Paper and pencil

1. Use a marker or pen to number about a dozen of the stickers. These will represent galaxies.

2. Blow up the balloon partway. Twist the end, double it over, and use a rubber band or twist tie to temporarily hold in the air. This will represent the space-time of a young universe.

3. Carefully place the numbered stickers on the inflated balloon. (It doesn't matter if you don't use them all, or if you need to number more.)

4. Measure and write down the distances between several of the numbered galaxies on your balloon universe. For example: 4→9 = 2 inches.

5. Now inflate the balloon, expanding the universe more. Close the balloon again and repeat step 4. What happens?

Think about it: What happens if, instead of using stickers as galaxies, you drew spirals on the balloon and inflated it? Why wouldn't this be a correct model for the expanding universe?

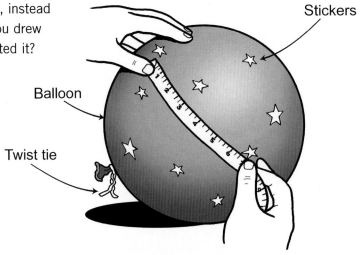

Stickers

Balloon

Twist tie

real—that all matter is actually scattering away from our region of space."

Those speeds led to a major discovery. In 1929 Edwin Hubble figured out that the farther away a galaxy is, the faster it moves—and the rate is proportional. In other words, a galaxy five times as far moves five times as fast. The equation is called **Hubble's Law**. The entire universe is stretching out, expanding like a balloon filling with air.

Albert Einstein's equations showing an unstable universe had been right after all—Hubble had proved it. On a winter day in 1931, Edwin Hubble escorted an aging Einstein up the winding road to Mount Wilson Observatory. The famous physicist wanted to see the magnificent 100-inch telescope for himself, and thank Edwin Hubble for his work there.

Edwin Hubble's observations of galaxies on the run matched Albert Einstein's equations of an expanding universe. But neither man's work explained *why* it was happening. It took a Catholic priest and mathematician from Belgium to put it all together—and then blow it apart.

Edwin Powell Hubble (1889–1953)

Edwin Powell Hubble was born in Marshfield, Missouri, at his grandparents' farmhouse. He was the third of seven kids raised by a stern father and encouraging mother. On the night of his eighth birthday, his grandfather showed him the stars through a telescope he'd set up. Edwin learned from his grandfather that the stars were faraway suns.

Edwin Hubble was an athletic boy who grew into a tall, strong teenager. He was good at sports, playing football and basketball, and set school records on the track team. Hubble liked the outdoors and fished and hiked his whole life. Edwin's high school grades earned him a scholarship to college, which he started at only 16. His father wanted Edwin to study law, but he took a different path. "I would rather be a second-rate astronomer than a first-rate lawyer," Hubble said. "All I want is astronomy."

Edwin Hubble went to work as an astronomer at the Mount Wilson Observatory in California in 1919. He worked there his whole life, studying nebulae, identifying and classifying galaxies, and discovering the expanding universe.

In 1990 **NASA** launched the *Hubble* Space Telescope, named in his honor. He would have supported the telescope's mission of continuing exploration. As Edwin Hubble said, "Equipped with his five senses, man explores the universe around him and calls the adventure science."

Edwin Powell Hubble in 1951. *NASA/STScI*

Monsignor Georges Henri Joseph Édouard Lemaître was a priest and a professor at the Catholic University of Louvain in Belgium.

AN EXPLOSIVE BEGINNING

Georges Lemaître (1894–1966) also volunteered for service in World War I. The young Belgian left engineering school for the battlefield in 1914. He was decorated for bravery, but the horror he'd seen drove him toward a religious life and he became a Catholic priest and a mathematician.

Lemaître had studied Einstein's theories. And when he read Hubble's discovery of an expanding universe, he began to wonder about the beginning of the cosmos. What could have started the expansion of the universe?

Lemaître thought about going backward, like rewinding a movie. The galaxies would get closer and closer until they came together and squashed into a single, tightly packed speck. His 1931 paper called it the "primeval atom" from which all matter blasted outward. The explosion of that ancient atom created the universe. The theory came to be called the Big Bang.

"The evolution of the world can be compared to a display of fireworks that has just ended," Lemaître wrote. "Some few red wisps, ashes and smoke. Standing on a cooled cinder, we see the slow fading of the suns, and we try to recall the vanishing brilliance of the origin of the worlds."

The **Big Bang theory** says that billions of years ago, a great explosion created all of space, matter, light, and even time. The clock of the cosmos starting ticking as all the stored energy in the explosion changed into matter. Einstein's $E = mc^2$ explains it, actually. An enormous eruption of energy flies apart, converting E into mass, or m. The earliest matter was just particles and atoms, but those eventually formed stars, solar systems, and planets.

Einstein himself wasn't convinced—not right away, at least. The Big Bang meant that the cosmos was unstable. He was in good company not liking that fact. Einstein and Lemaître met a number of times in the early 1930s. The two men discussed physics, mathematics, and the Big Bang. Then, in 1935, Einstein was in the audience during a presentation given by Lemaître. When it ended, Einstein stood up, applauded, and said, "This is the most beautiful and satisfactory explanation of creation to which I have ever listened."

At particle accelerators, such as this one in Europe, researchers send atomic particles to the speed of light and smash them together, creating mini Big Bangs and studying the creation of matter. *CERN*

5

1930s–1970s:
Discovering the Invisible:
Quasars, Pulsars, and Black Holes

Karl Jansky felt lucky to land a job with Bell Telephone Laboratories in 1928. The physicist had finished college and hit the job market just as the Great Depression set in. Jansky wasn't going to complain when Bell Labs assigned him to a remote site in "the sticks" of northeastern New Jersey.

The pioneering research company had been leery about hiring Jansky. The thin, young man had Bright's disease, a chronic kidney disorder. Bell Labs decided that a country setting would be less stressful for Jansky than its headquarters in New York City. With a salary of $33 a week, Karl Jansky started studying the noisy static that tormented telephone callers. He ended up discovering a whole new way to explore the universe.

STARRY STATIC

In the 1930s, a call from New York to London traveled on **radio waves** over the ocean. (Underwater telephone cables weren't laid until the 1950s.) These transatlantic radiotelephone calls sounded terrible. The radio signals were full of static from electrical equipment and bad weather. Before engineers could deal with this interference, Bell Labs needed to know exactly what caused it. Figuring out where all the noisy static came from was Karl Jansky's job.

To track down the interference in the airways, Jansky built a giant, odd-looking antennae. It was a barebones wooden frame as big as a barn and had brass piping strung with wires. The whole contraption was mounted on four Ford Model T wheels and sat on a round track so that it could be rotated. Jansky called it his merry-go-round.

By 1932 the antennae was picking up static from local thunderstorms, faraway storms in the tropics—and an unidentified natural noisemaker. Jansky described the mysterious sound as "a very steady hiss type static, the origin of which is not yet known." The static was too weak to bother radiotelephones, but Karl Jansky was curious anyway. His father, a professor of engineering, had taught his children to question everything. What could be causing the constant hiss?

The Sun seemed like a probable answer. The static ebbed and flowed about every 24 hours, after all. Months of studying the strange sound's direction showed it wasn't coming from the Sun, however. It had to be coming from farther out in space. In a 1933 letter to his father, Karl Jansky wrote, "Have you any idea what could be the actual source of these noise waves? I've been giving my imagination free rein, but without result as yet. I imagine that it will take an astrono-mer who knows something about the outer regions of space to answer that question."

Astronomers were also stumped by the discovery, but not inspired to investigate it. So Jansky kept listening. The 28-year-old physicist realized that the static was stron-gest when he pointed the antennae at the constellation Sagittarius, toward the star-packed center of our galaxy. Then he realized the source—the Milky Way itself! Stars were

This reconstruction of Karl Jansky's first radio telescope was built on the grounds of the National Radio Astronomy Observatory in Green Bank, West Virginia. *Jarek Tuszynski*

making the static by giving off radio waves. The densest region of stars was the noisiest. Jansky called it "star noise."

On May 5, 1933, a headline in the *New York Times* read NEW RADIO WAVES TRACED TO THE CENTER OF THE MILKY WAY. Reporters listened to a sample of Jansky's "star noise," saying it sounded "like steam escaping from a radiator."

Astronomers were less intrigued. Most doubted the Milky Way could put out such intense radio waves. Nor did many astrono-mers comprehend what radio waves from the

cosmos might tell them about the universe. How could an antenna make discoveries, like telescopes do? What could it possibly "see"?

Jansky's cosmic radio waves didn't inter-fere with telephone calls, so Bell Labs didn't want to fund the research. Money was tight during the Great Depression. Bell Labs reas-signed Karl Jansky and he worked on other projects until he passed away at age 44 from kidney failure.

By following up on his curiosity, Karl Jansky started a new science: **radio astron-**

omy. It took a while to get started. World War II came and went before astronomers embraced it. But studying radio waves coming from and bouncing off space objects has given us a new view of the universe. Radio waves cut through the gas and dust of space, giving astronomers a clearer picture of stars and galaxies. Karl Jansky died without ever hearing the term radio astronomy, but it was his discovery that started it.

LIGHT SEEN AND UNSEEN

Radio astronomy opened a window on what was once unseen and unimaginable in the universe. Objects no one knew existed suddenly appeared when viewed with a radio telescope. Soon astronomers started trying to glimpse the invisible up in the sky in all sorts of ways—ultraviolet, infrared, X-rays, etc. Astronomers began seeing the universe in a new light by studying all its different

Karl Guthe Jansky (1905–1950).
Image courtesy of NRAO/AUI

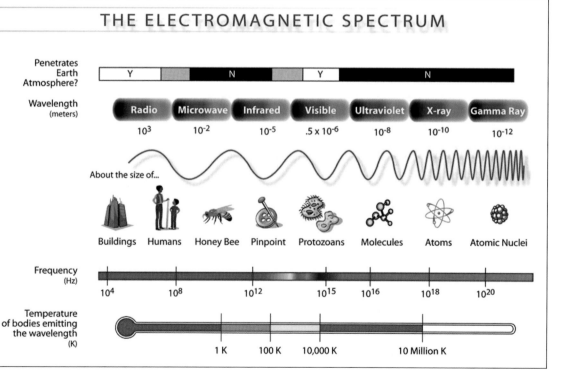

Wavelength, frequency, and temperature are related along the spectrum of types of electromagnetic radiation. Radio waves are big, low frequency, and cool compared to short, fast, hot gamma rays. *NASA*

Track Down Interference

activity

Radio astronomers study the radio waves coming from faraway cosmic objects such as comets, exploding stars, and black holes. These signals are faint and difficult to collect from such distant sources. All our modern devices add to the challenge. Electronic games, remote-control toys, cell phones, digital cameras, and vehicles all churn out signals that radio telescopes pick up. Human-created radio waves like these are called radio frequency interference or RFI. Similar to how nighttime lit-up cities create light pollution for optical telescopes, RFI is signal pollution for radio telescopes. Radio astronomy observatories must quiet the skies near them by limiting the electronics in the area.

Are the skies around you quiet enough for a radio telescope? Or is there too much RFI clogging up the airways? Find out by making and using your own RFI detector.

YOU'LL NEED

⇒ Small AA battery

⇒ Small scrap of cardboard or old magazine

⇒ Heavy tape

⇒ Piece of insulated wire with two bare ends

⇒ Portable radio with AM band

⇒ Paper and pencil

1. Lay a small battery on a scrap of cardboard. Tape it down so both ends remain exposed. Bend an insulated wire into a horseshoe or U shape. Make sure the insulation is stripped off both ends, but only the ends.

2. Turn on a radio and choose the AM band. Tune the radio to the low (left) end of the frequencies, where there are fewer stations. Set it near the battery.

3. Hold the bent wire in the center where it's insulated with both hands. Move the wire so both bare ends touch the top and bottom of the battery. (Note: It needs to be bare wire touching the battery.) Try to maneuver one side of the wire so it touches the battery and then make the other end of the wire tap against the other end of the battery to complete the circuit. **DO NOT** touch the bare wire or the battery; they can get hot.

4. Listen for the static, or RFI, coming through the radio. Tune the radio

up and down, changing the signal's frequency. Does that make a difference in the noise you hear?

5. Now that you know what static sounds like, put your radio to work as a RFI detector. Make a chart to record your findings. It needs three columns, with these headings:

   Object   RFI Noise   RFI Level (1–5)

6. Turn on the AM radio and listen for RFI near different electronic devices. Record your findings on the chart, including what the RFI noise sounds like (pulses, scratching, etc.) for each object and how loud the RFI level is from 1 to 5, with 5 being very loud. Some possible objects to check: cell phones, remote-control toys, electric shavers, microwave ovens, TVs, and handheld video games.

Portable radio

Cardboard

Insulated wire

AA battery

Think about it: What objects made the most static? The least?

These 82-feet-in-diameter (25 m) radio antennae make up the Very Large Array (VLA) radio astronomy observatory in New Mexico. Data from the 27-dish antennae is combined, making it an overall 22-mile-wide (36 km) radio telescope. *Tom Uhlman Photography*

kinds of light—not just **visible light**, the kind the human eye sees and regular **optical telescopes** gather, but the entire **electromagnetic spectrum**.

All light, visible and invisible, is **electromagnetic (EM) radiation**, the vibrating waves of electric and magnetic fields that travel at the speed of light (186,000 miles per second, or 300,000 km/sec). **Gamma rays**,

X-rays, **ultraviolet light**, **infrared light**, **microwaves**, and radio waves are EM radiation, too. They may be invisible to you, but they exist.

Think about infrared light, which is heat. Soldiers use special infrared night goggles to see heat emitted by living bodies and warm machinery in the dark. X-ray light reveals scissors in luggage or broken bones inside

a medical patient. Crime scene investigators use ultraviolet light to look for invisible clues, such as washed-off blood. Detecting light in the whole EM spectrum gives us different ways and means of seeing what's there.

Objects in space give off many kinds of EM radiation, and each type of light has its own wavelength, **frequency**, and energy. Gamma rays have the shortest wavelength and radio waves have the longest.

Electromagnetic radiation is not only waves, but also particles of energy called **photons**. The energy of a photon depends on its wavelength and frequency. Radiation that has a short wavelength has a high frequency, and also high energy that makes it hot. Radiation such as radio waves, with a long wavelength, has a low frequency and low energy so is cool. The characteristics of different kinds of EM radiation are useful to astronomers because they can tell them the conditions that produced the specific kind of electromagnetic radiation. What makes something give off heat, like a fire, is very different from something that creates gamma rays, like a nuclear reactor.

The long waves of radio emissions cut through the dust and gas of space. They pass easily through our **atmosphere**. This means that radio telescopes can be built nearly anywhere, not just on mountaintops, where optical telescopes must be. A radio telescope looks like a giant dish antenna, or a group of them spread over many acres on the ground. Above Earth's atmosphere is where ultraviolet, X-ray, and gamma-ray telescopes do their work. The shorter waves of these kinds of EM radiation can't penetrate our thick air. The first X-ray and ultraviolet telescopes traveled above the atmosphere on rockets or airplanes. Orbiting **satellites** later made long-term telescope observation of X-ray, ultraviolet, and gamma rays possible.

Studying the kinds, amounts, and patterns of EM radiation that space objects emit can tell astronomers a lot about them. For example, the hottest objects in space produce X-rays and the highest energy areas make gamma rays. And sometimes astronomers looking at what's invisible find something entirely new in the universe.

QUASI-STELLAR RADIO

By the late 1950s radio telescopes scanned the skies, listening for radio frequencies coming from distant objects. Ever-improving radio telescopes were finding thousands of radio sources, helping to pinpoint new objects in space.

Astronomers worked to match up those sources with visible objects. Many were big, elliptical galaxies with jets of radio waves, called **radio galaxies**, but a few seemed much smaller. Maarten Schmidt took up the challenge in 1962. The young Dutch astronomer wanted to figure out what in the universe these small radio-gushing dim objects were. All he needed was a closer look. That meant using the biggest optical telescope in the world.

The Hale telescope sits inside a huge white dome atop Palomar Mountain in California. Its 200-inch mirror made it the largest telescope for many decades after its completion in 1948. The Hale telescope remains one of the world's biggest, even today.

The Arecibo radio telescope in Puerto Rico is the world's largest. Its "dish" covers about 20 acres and is made of 40,000 connected panels that are suspended in a natural sinkhole.

Courtesy of the National Astronomy and Ionosphere Center, Arecibo Observatory, a facility of the National Science Foundation, photo by Robert Parker

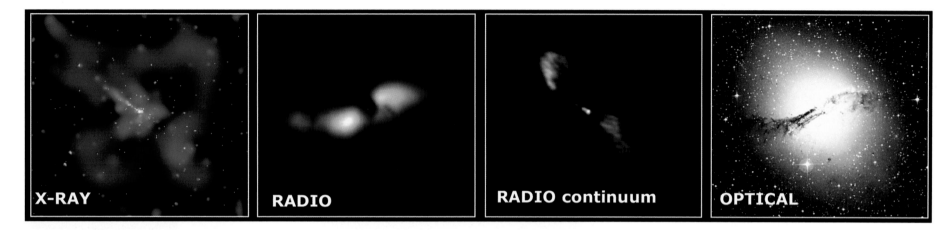

X-RAY   **RADIO**   **RADIO continuum**   **OPTICAL**

Above: These images are all of Centaurus A, a galaxy about 11 million light-years from Earth in the constellation Centaurus. Each image reveals the galaxy in a different wavelength of light. X-ray *(NASA/CXC/M. Karovska et al.)*; Radio 21-cm image *(NRAO/VLA/J. Van Gorkom/Schminovich et al.)*; Radio continuum image *(NRAO/VLA/J. Condon et al.)*; Optical *(Digitized Sky Survey U.K. Schmidt Image/STScI)*

Left: The 200-inch Hale Telescope at Palomar Observatory. *NASA*

Make a Radio Picture

activity

Radio waves are invisible, so how do radio astronomers turn them into images like those of Centaurus on page 81? A radio telescope focuses on and collects the invisible waves from space. It converts the waves into a signal that a computer records and stores. It's the information in these signals that becomes the images you see.

See for yourself how signal information can become a picture.

YOU'LL NEED

➤ Graph paper (or use a ruler to draw a 30-by-20 square grid on a sheet of white paper)

➤ Colored pencils or markers in black, blue, red, brown, green, and yellow

1. Look at the picture below, made with a grid of squares. It's similar to pixels on a computer or TV screen. The computer knows which color to display by a code. In this example, each pixel space has a single number that translates into a color. Blank or white is 0, black is 1, blue is 2, green is 3, red is 4, brown is 5, and yellow is 6.

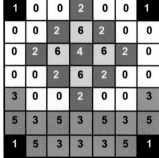

2. What does it look like? (Looking at it from a distance can help!) The more pixels, the higher the resolution, and the sharper the image. If this flower was on a grid with 100 by 100 squares, it would be a lot clearer.

3. Ready to decode a picture with a lot more pixels? On a sheet of graph paper, outline a grid 30 squares wide by 20 squares tall. (You can also create your own grid with a ruler and pen on white paper.)

4. Starting from the left, fill in the top row of squares with the letters of the alphabet, starting with A. Because there are 30 spaces, you'll need to use AA, BB, CC, and DD after Z.

5. Use a pencil to fill in the 30 lettered columns with the following strings of numbers. One number in each box, going down the column. (This is easier with a friend. One person can call out the numbers and the other can write them in.)

A: 22222211222222112222; B: 22222213122221312222; C: 22222216312213612222;
D: 22222216311136122222; E: 22222213633631222222; F: 22222222166661222222;
G: 22222222166612222222; H: 22222222213612222222; I: 22222222133331222222;
J: 22222221336312222222; K: 22222213333331222222; L: 22222221336363122222;
M: 22222216333333612222; N: 22221333566533312222; O: 22221363333333631222;
P: 22111333366663331222; Q: 21111333335533333122; R: 21111333666666333112;
S: 22113333555533333112; T: 22213366666666633122; U: 22211333333333331122;
V: 20221333333333331222; W: 22221333553333331222; X: 20221335015343312222;
Y: 22222135115343122222; Z: 22022213553341222222; AA: 22222213333341222222;
BB: 22220221111112222222; CC: 22222222211222222222; DD: 22222222222222222222

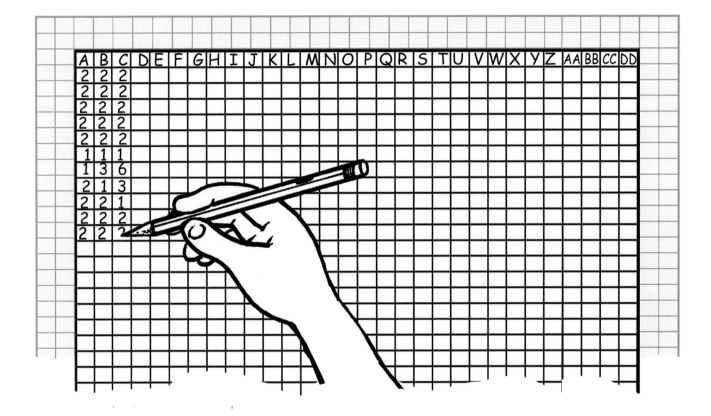

6. Once all the squares are numbered, color in each square according to the code in step 1. What image appears from your data?

7. Now create your own coded image. Draw a pixel picture on graph paper using colored pencils or pens. Give each color a number and fill in the squares with the correct numbers. Then turn the whole thing into code by writing out strings of numbers for each row, as in step 5. Challenge a friend to break the code and reveal your image!

Using the telescope in the early 1960s was a bit like taking a space flight. In the evening, Maarten Schmidt would enter the giant dome and shimmy into a heated flight suit. Then a slow elevator began hauling him toward the ceiling. His destination was a big metal tube, called the observer's cage. Once

Maarten Schmidt (left) next to the Wurzburg antenna at Radio Kootwijk, Holland, sometime between 1952 and 1955.

Netherlands Institute of Radio Astronomy (ASTRON)

settled in for his night shift, the great doors of the dome opened. Cold mountain air rushed in as the telescope swung into place and Maarten Schmidt got to work.

Schmidt, like so many astronomers before him, caught the stargazing bug as a kid. The view through his uncle's telescope transfixed

Maarten at age 12. By the time he was in high school, teachers were letting him give the astronomy lessons. Maarten Schmidt's father thought it was all going a bit too far once his son was in college. "How can you earn your daily bread by looking at the stars?" he would ask his son.

Maarten stuck with the stars though, becoming an assistant to famous astronomer and fellow Dutchman Jan Oort before moving to California permanently. The big telescopes at Palomar Observatory are addictive, explained Schmidt: "Once you've worked with them, it's hard not to return."

Maarten Schmidt spent many nights during the winter of 1962 and 1963 in the chilly cage up in the Hale dome. He was focusing on a couple of the mysterious, dim, radio wave–making objects, including one with the identification number 3C 273. It was a blue starlike object in the constellation Virgo that emitted a huge amount of energy in intense radio waves. What was 3C 273, exactly?

Schmidt studied the object's spectrum for clues. The dim point of light might seem like a star, but its spectrum was like no other star he'd ever seen. Schmidt puzzled over the plates showing the spectral lines. Then it hit him. "A redshift," he realized. "And immediately it struck me how incredible it was," Schmidt remembered. "How could a star exhibit a big redshift?"

It couldn't. Seeing the big redshift meant that 3C 273 wasn't a star at all! Astronomers knew that stars don't redshift like that. They don't zoom away fast enough to stretch their wavelengths from blue to red, like the lowering tone of a passing car stereo. Seeing a redshift of that size takes looking through great distances. Only far-off galaxies can have their light waves so lengthened by the expansion of the universe.

Using the amount of redshift and the object's brightness, Maarten Schmidt calculated that 3C 273 is 3 billion light-years away. In 1963 it was the farthest object ever seen. And it was 5 trillion times as bright as the Sun. Plus, it was speeding away at an unimaginable 30,000 miles (48,000 km) per second. "I was in a state of complete shock," remembered Schmidt. Discovering something new in the universe will do that to you.

FROM QUASAR TO PULSAR

Astronomers began calling the small, bright, distant objects Schmidt had discovered "quasi-stellar radio sources," or **quasars**. As the name hints, no one actually knew yet what they were. But quasars were getting a lot of attention anyway.

A young British research student at Cambridge was soon studying them, too. "Quasars were very important things at that

Left: Maarten Schmidt's discovery got him on the cover of *Time* magazine in 1966 with the banner "Exploring the Edge of the Universe."
Tom Uhlman Photography

Right: The first quasar discovered, 3C 273, imaged in 2003 by the *Hubble* Space Telescope.
NASA, M. Clampin (STScI), H. Ford (JHU), G. Illingworth (UCO/ Lick Observatory), J. Krist (STScI), D. Ardila (JHU), D. Golimowski (JHU), the ACS Science Team, J. Bahcall (IAS) and ESA

Above: The Four-Acre Array radio telescope near Cambridge, England, where pulsars were discovered. *Graham Woan*

Right: Jocelyn Bell-Burnell in 1977. *NASA*

time," said Jocelyn Bell. "Maarten Schmidt had just identified the red shift of the first one. It was realized that they were very, very distant." Before she could study quasars, Bell and her radio astronomy colleagues at Cambridge needed to build a telescope to find them.

Unlike some radio telescopes, what came to be called the Four-Acre Array is not a giant dish radio telescope. It is made up of 1,000 wooden posts spread out over the area of 60 tennis courts with 100 miles of cable and wire connected between them. Wandering sheep keep the grass under control. "We did the work ourselves and cheerfully sledgehammered all one summer," said Bell.

Jocelyn Bell was set on being a radio astronomer. She wanted to put the physics she'd studied in college to use exploring the universe. "I was grabbed by the sheer scale and splendor of the field, of the cosmos, the sizes, the quantities . . . and also the number of beautiful pictures of galaxies in books," said Bell. Now that astronomers were identifying radio galaxies, she wondered how they related to beautiful spiral galaxies like our own.

By late 1967 the Four-Acre Array radio telescope was ready to find quasars and measure their sizes. The idea was to identify quasars by the twinkling of their radio signals. Just as starlight twinkles as it passes through Earth's swirling atmosphere, radio waves from quasars are also jostled passing through **solar wind** streaming from the Sun.

Bell was in charge of operating the expansive telescope, and sorting through the 96 feet of paper charts the data recorder spat out daily. The 24-year-old analyzed the charts with her eyes, not with computers. After a few days Bell learned to recognize the patterns of peaks and valleys the recorders' swinging pens traced on the charts. She could easily separate the twinkling quasars from static. So far, so good. Then something odd turned up.

SCRUFFY ALIEN SIGNALS

"Six or eight weeks after starting the survey I became aware that on occasions there was a bit of 'scruff' on the records," remembered Bell. She meant the Irish version of "scruff"—untidy clutter or something out of place. In other words, something that

This image of the Crab Nebula in X-ray and other wavelengths of light shows the gas and matter spinning and shooting out from the pulsar. *NASA/CXC/ASU/J. Hester et al., HST/ASU/J. Hester et al.*

was not a twinkling quasar or interference. "Furthermore, I realized that this scruff had been seen before on the same part of the records—from the same patch of sky." Bell made the recorder faster, to tune in on the scruff. "As the chart flowed under the pen I could see that the signal was a series of

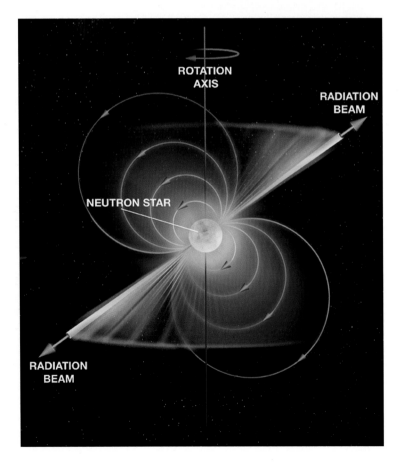

A pulsar spins out a beam of radiation, including radio waves, generated by a neutron star. *B. Saxton/NRAO/AUI*

ROTATION AXIS

RADIATION BEAM

NEUTRON STAR

RADIATION BEAM

pulses," said Bell. Perfectly equally spaced pulses that were 1.337 seconds apart.

Jocelyn Bell's supervisor, Tony Hewish, suspected the peculiar pulses were from a human-made source. They were too fast and steady to be twinkling quasars. Orbiting satellites were investigated—then ruled out.

Then French television signals, radar bouncing off the moon, and static from a nearby large, metal building were looked into as possible sources—and rejected.

What about aliens? Were the pulses signals from a civilization beyond Earth? The idea that "some silly lot of little green men" might be messing up her research irritated Jocelyn Bell. Fortunately for her project, she found similar pulsations coming from three other batches of sky soon after. It seemed unlikely that four different alien species would be trying to talk to Earth at the same time.

If not aliens, then what? A young Italian astronomer had the final puzzle piece. Franco Pacini wrote a paper giving a reason why the Crab Nebula was still so bright and full of energy 1,000 years after the star became a **supernova**. Pacini suggested that a kind of **neutron star** could be powering the Crab Nebula. A neutron star is a star that died in a supernova explosion so intense that the star's core melded into a ball of uncharged subatomic particles—neutrons. This space ball of neutrons is dense and heavy beyond belief. While a typical neutron star is the size of a city, more matter than is contained the Sun is squashed into it. A neutron star is a kind of star zombie—dead but full of energy.

Pacini predicted that the neutron star in the Crab Nebula was rapidly rotating and has a strong magnetic field. This is where its energy came from, Pacini argued. Researchers studying the Crab Nebula soon found the star remnant at its heart. And it was beating with pulses at the same rate as those Bell recorded at the Four-Acre Array. The energy-creating object in the Crab Nebula and Bell's mystery sources of pulsations were the same—and something entirely different. They'd discovered "pulsating radio sources," or **pulsars**, an entirely new citizen of the cosmos.

Pulsars were a brand new kind of space object. A pulsar is a small, spinning, super-dense neutron star that emits a massive magnetic field. Pulsars are the largest magnets in the universe. A pulsar-sized magnet halfway to the moon could pull a metal pen from your pocket. The magnetic field of fast-spinning pulsars shoots out radiation, including intense beams of radio waves that

Make a Pulsar — activity

Pulsars are small, spinning, dense neutron stars with incredibly strong magnetic fields. Pulsars shoot out beams of radiation that are swept around as it spins. On Earth, we pick up that beam of radio waves, light, and other electromagnetic radiation in a pulse or flash as it sweeps across us.

Like the light inside a lighthouse, a pulsar constantly beams radiation from its hot spots. But because of its **rotation**, it reaches us in pulses. You can model the effect with a friend, two flashlights, and a swivel chair.

Ask your friend to sit on the chair with a flashlight in each hand. Have the friend hold out his or her arms in a T with both flashlights on. Turn off the room lights and tell the friend to start spinning. What do you see?

stream through space. "The beam is swept around as the pulsar rotates," explained Bell. "It's like a lighthouse. When the beam sweeps across us, we pick up a pulse or a flash."

FROM PULSAR TO BLACK HOLES

Jocelyn Bell's survey of quasars in 1967 led to the discovery of pulsars and their magnetic source of radio pulses. Massive stars have violent, explosive deaths, and some leave behind neutron stars and pulsars. The super-dense makeup of these powerful star zombies creates an incredible amount of gravity. Think of the warping a pulsar causes as it sinks deeply into the grid of space-time. Light itself is curved and bent as it escapes out of the space-time well.

Now imagine an object leftover from an even bigger supernova, one that has even more mass squeezed into its small size than a neutron star. This shrunken, dead star's gravity is so powerful that nothing can travel fast enough to escape it—not even light. What has so much gravity that it creates a light-trapping sinkhole in space-time? A black hole.

Astronomers have long speculated about such objects. After Einstein set the speed

Engineers prepare the X-ray explorer satellite named *Uhuru* for launch in 1970. *NASA*

limit of light, the German physicist Karl Schwarzschild took the next step. He figured that if light can only go so fast, then something with sufficient gravity can keep light from going forward. Like the escape velocity of a rocket, more speed is needed to break free of a bigger planet. Something 25 times as heavy as the Sun maxes out the speed of light's ability to reach escape velocity at all.

Schwarzschild imagined a dark, light-trapping, bottomless throat or cone.

Physicist John Wheeler came up with a catchy name in 1967—a black hole. The name is fitting: it is black from its lack of light and a hole in space-time into which things can fall.

The idea of a lightless object is one thing. Finding a black hole is quite another. How do you find something that traps all light? You look for what it's doing. The gravity of black holes affects the space around them. It tugs at nearby objects, such as stars. And the black hole itself funnels in the gas and dust around it. The pulled-in space stuff swirls toward the black hole at nearly light speed. The accelerating atoms in the dust and gas heat up and give off X-rays and other high-energy light. By looking for hot, swirling material in space and other effects that may have a black hole to blame, astronomers can track them down.

A small satellite with the Swahili name *Uhuru* helped uncover the first observed black hole. *Uhuru* was the first ever-orbiting X-ray telescope. Its name means "freedom" in the language of Kenya—the country

from which the NASA satellite launched in late 1970. The small *Uhuru* satellite scanned the sky for signs of explosive X-ray energy. It found hundreds of sources, including Cygnus X-1 in the Swan (Cygnus) constellation.

Astronomers on the ground began turning their telescopes toward the X-ray source. In 1971 astronomers Louise Webster and Paul Murdin were looking in Cygnus X-1's direction from London's Royal Greenwich Observatory. They saw a hot blue star 20 times the size of the Sun.

Paul Murdin suspected that Cygnus X-1 might have a connection to this blue star. "We did not think there was anything about it that would cause it to emit X-rays," wrote Murdin. "However, we thought that its motion would change if it was circling around an X-ray companion."

After tracking the blue star, Webster and Murdin found that the blue star was indeed moving around a companion. There are lots of binary stars that orbit each other—that's not unusual. But this companion star was unseen and unseeable. "We had discovered that the other X-ray emitting star in Cygnus

X-1 is actually a black hole," wrote Murdin. It was the first black hole ever observed.

Cygnus X-1 was likely a large star that went supernova, collapsing into matter so dense that its gravity keeps light from escaping. Its companion star survived and is now continually dragged around its black hole form. Cygnus X-1 now feeds on its binary partner. The black hole pulls a continual stream of the star's gases toward it, swirling them into a fiery disc as it swallows, squeezes, heats the matter, and burps out X-rays.

FROM BLACK HOLES TO QUASARS

Black holes are places in space where the force of gravity has crushed an incredible amount of matter into a small space. Sometimes this happens, as with Cygnus X-1, when a giant star dies and shrinks into a dense ball.

Where else is a whole bunch of matter squeezed together really tightly? In the center of large galaxies. This is where supermassive black holes lurk. In 1969, Donald Lynden-Bell argued that black holes are at the center of most of the massive galaxies in the universe. The English astrophysicist figured this out by studying quasars.

Nearly 10 years after Maarten Schmidt had discovered them, quasars were still only quasi-understood. What exactly were these far-off, fast-moving, high-energy, galaxy-like things? What was generating all that light, radio, and other EM radiation?

Donald Lynden-Bell claimed that the power behind quasars comes from the disc of stuff around the edge of a black hole.

This is an illustration of the black hole Cygnus X-1 (left) and its blue star companion (right). The black hole pulls in gas from the star, swirling the matter into a hot red and orange disc on its way into the black hole or burning up the matter into powerful jets of radiation. *NASA/CXC/M.Weiss*

The Crown Prince Haakon of Norway presents Maarten Schmidt (left) and Donald Lynden-Bell (middle) with the 2008 Kavli Prize for Astrophysics for discovering quasars and their source.

Hakon Mosvold Larsen/Scanpix

Supermassive black holes power these bright centers of galaxies called quasars. Supermassive black holes aren't the same as black holes made by supernova explosions. Black holes like Cygnus X-1 are tiny in comparison to a supermassive black hole, which can have a billion times the mass of the Sun. "They're monster gravitational bodies that eat their environment," explained Maarten Schmidt, the discoverer of quasars. The mass gobbled down the throat of a supermassive black hole gives it energy. Quasars are hungry, young galaxies, born soon after the Big Bang. Gravity at the center of a newborn galaxy squashes the stars and gas clouds together, crushing them into a supermassive black hole.

Quasars are energized by stuff being pulled into supermassive black holes. All those bits of swirling dust and gas hit, scrape, and chafe each other. This friction creates heat, like two hands rubbing together. When the hot matter slides into the black hole, it explodes into X-rays that heat up the disc. This huge, hot, spinning disc around the black hole glows with ultraviolet and visible light: a quasar.

Quasars are some of the most distant objects in space. There aren't any in our old space neighborhood. The galaxies nearest Earth have grown up, and the supermassive black holes at their centers have already eaten most of what there is. The supermassive black holes are still there—nearly every galaxy likely has one at its center. Older supermassive black holes are harder to see. "Whether you see them or not depends entirely on whether it is eating or not," explained Schmidt. "It may be a billion solar masses, like that in a quasar, or it may be small, like the one in the Milky Way."

That's right, there is a supermassive black hole about 26,000 light-years from us. Its name is Sagittarius A*. (It's in the constellation Sagittarius, like the radio signal that Karl Jansky picked up in 1932.) Our galaxy's supermassive black hole is only about 14 million miles (22.5 million km) across. But while Sagittarius A* could fit between the Sun and Mercury, it has as much mass as 2 to 4 million suns.

The middle decades of the 20th century revised our view of the universe. It grew in size and complexity, as new objects were discovered and old objects rediscovered in a new light. The idea of a peaceful sky of twinkling stars was abandoned. The quiet was broken. The universe is a violent place, full of explosions and X-rays, giant spinning magnets shooting out radio waves, and galaxy-devouring black holes. What else might be lurking out there?

SGR A*

Right: This is an image of the supermassive black hole at the center of the Milky Way called Sagittarius A* taken by the orbiting *Chandra* X-Ray Observatory. *NASA/CXC/MIT/F.K. Baganoff et al.*

Cosmic Background Noise

Tracking down the source of unknown noise led to discoveries beyond radio astronomy and pulsars. Pesky static led astronomers to discover the energy left over from our universe's creation.

In 1964, physicists Arno Penzias and Robert Wilson (like Karl Jansky before them) were working at Bell Labs. The pair wanted to detect radio waves coming from the halo of gas around the Milky Way's center. They hoped an odd-shaped radio antenna would be sensitive enough to pick up the radio signal. But after a year of tweaking, they'd been unable to get rid of certain sources of interference. The faint electromagnetic radiation was coming from all directions in space.

Unable to figure out what it was, Penzias and Wilson asked around for ideas. It turned out that they'd stumbled on exactly what others had been searching for. Their interference was actually a glow of microwaves from the entire universe—**cosmic microwave background radiation**.

Cosmic microwave background (CMB) radiation is the afterglow of our universe's explosive start. After the Big Bang, the hot universe cooled down. CMB is the leftover radiation from that explosion, which happened 13.7 billion years ago! The discovery of CMB was powerful evidence to support the Big Bang theory. Added to Edwin Hubble's discovery of an expanding universe, it disproved those who argued that the universe is unchanging. The Big Bang became not just a theory, but the accepted history of the birth of the universe.

The so-called horn antenna that Robert Wilson (left) and Arno Penzias (right) used to discover cosmic microwave background. *Alcatel-Lucent/Bell Labs*

Make a Black Hole

activity

All objects that have mass warp and dent space-time. A black hole is something so massive that it deeply dents space-time into a sort of bottomless well. The sides of the well are so steep that not even light can escape. Black holes so powerfully distort space-time that they swallow up whatever is close by. The more massive and powerful the black hole, the farther its pull reaches.

YOU'LL NEED

➡ Balloon

➡ Scissors

➡ Metal can

➡ Rubber band

➡ Glitter of various colors and sizes

➡ Pencil with eraser

1. Cut a balloon in half across its middle. Then cover the open end of a can with it.

2. Use a rubber band to secure the balloon tightly across the can's end. The balloon rubber should be smooth, with no wrinkles, but not so tight that it'll easily tear.

3. The rubber-covered top of the can will represent the flexible fabric of space-time. Evenly scatter some glitter of different sizes onto the rubber-covered top. These particles will represent stars, dust, and other space matter.

4. Dent space-time like a black hole does by gently pushing the eraser end of the pencil an inch (2.5 cm) down into the center of the space-time fabric. What happens to the space-matter glitter when space-time is dented? Why?

5. Brush off the glitter. Repeat steps 3 and 4, pushing the eraser twice as deep into the space-time fabric. Why is more distant space-matter affected this time?

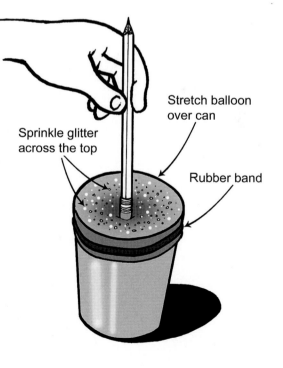

Sprinkle glitter across the top

Stretch balloon over can

Rubber band

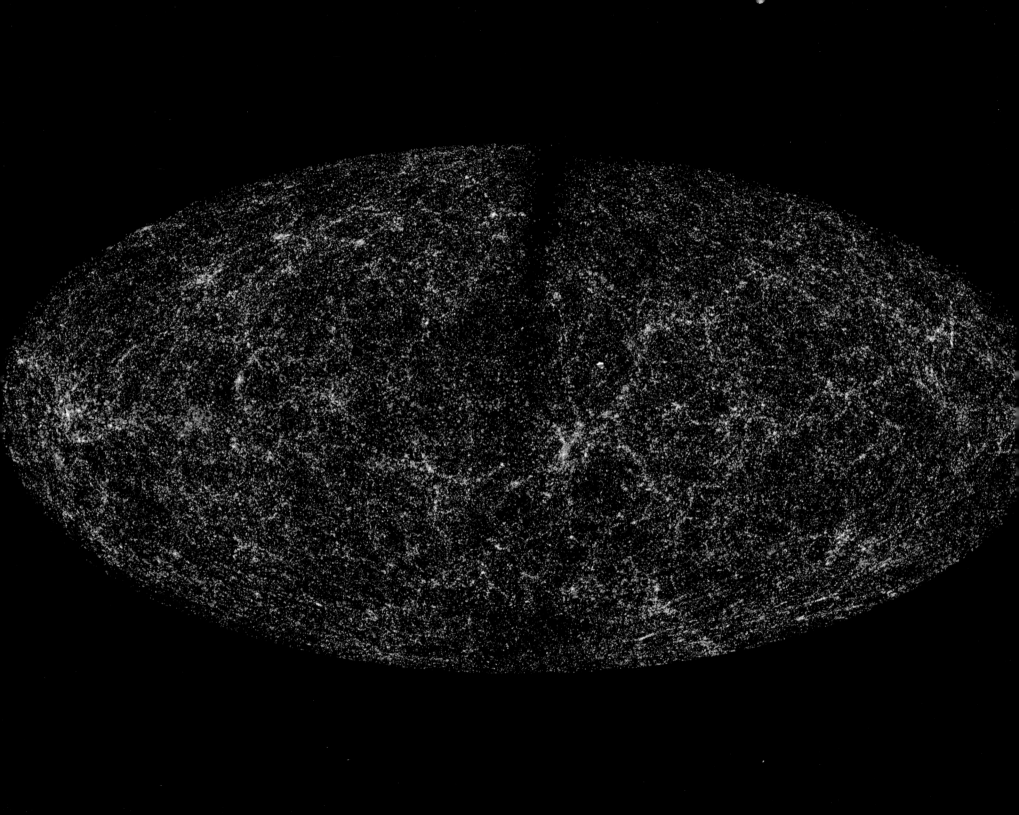

6

1980s–2010s: Frothy Galaxies, Alien Planets, and Dark Energy

This map of 1.6 million galaxies shows the three-dimensional structure of the nearby universe. The brightest and nearest galaxies, clusters, and **superclusters** are blue and the fainter, more distant ones are red.

Two Micron All-Sky Survey

Margaret Geller studies galaxies. Not individual ones, but groups of them, called clusters. The astrophysicist investigates galaxy clusters to find out how they form, change, and arrange themselves within our universe.

When she started out in the 1970s, most scientists believed that the universe was a uniform place. There were scattered clusters or clumps of galaxies here or there, but any unevenness disappeared at a distance. Just as a shirt's pinstripes blend into a single color from far away, the universe also looks the same from any distant position. At least that's what astronomers thought.

In the 1980s new imaging technology—the kind in today's digital cameras—changed how astronomers work. Unlike photographs from film, digital image recorders are sensitive enough to capture the spectra of very distant galaxies. By spreading out this galaxy light into colors,

like a prism, the amount of redshift can be precisely measured. How much the light has shifted to the red end of the spectrum tells astronomers how far away the galaxy is.

Measuring distances this way forever changed our maps of the cosmos. Maps went from two-dimensional, flat pictures of what can be seen to three-dimensional models that chart where galaxies actually are. Astronomers soon realized that the universe looks very different in three dimensions. Galaxies no longer looked so evenly spread out. Researchers began finding huge, dark, empty regions in space. The universe could no longer be considered uniform.

SOAP BUBBLES OF STARS

"One of the great challenges of modern cosmology," said Margaret Geller, "is to discover what the geometry of the universe really is." Geller and her coworker John Huchra

Margaret J. Geller is a pioneer in mapping the nearby universe. *SAO*

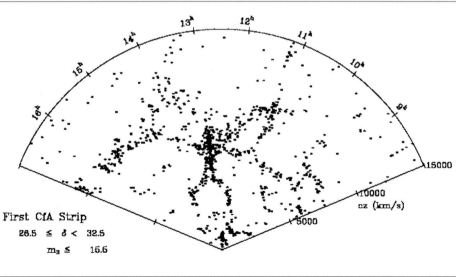

The magical first slice of galaxies mapped by Margaret Geller in 1986, nicknamed the Stick Man. *SAO*

First CfA Strip

$26.5 \leq \delta < 32.5$

$m_B \leq 15.5$

set out to do just that in the mid-1980s. Truthfully, both doubted the claims of huge, empty, dark regions without galaxies. So they started a survey of galaxies in a pie-shaped slice of the sky. They mapped all the galaxies they could see in their chosen wedge of space using the 1.5-meter telescope on Mount Hopkins in Arizona.

In the first year, they measured the distances and positions of 1,000 galaxies. Then the galaxies were plotted into the team's first map. Those once-doubtful voids of empty space were plainly there—and more.

Margaret Geller experienced an unforgettable feeling the first time she looked at the simple map. All of the empty regions had a similar round, bubble-like shape to them. The globular voids were also nested together, like bubbles squeezed into a box. And the 200-million-light-years-across bubbles of darkness were covered in a fabric of glowing galaxies.

"It was a kind of magic," Geller said. "The pattern of galaxies in our three-dimensional slice of the universe suggested that sheets, or walls, containing thousands of galaxies mark the boundaries of vast dark regions nearly devoid of galaxies," Geller wrote. "The patterns in the universe are similar to a household sponge or to bubbles in the kitchen sink enlarged about a thousand trillion trillion times."

The magic of science started for Margaret Geller as a child. Her father was a chemist. He studied how atoms arrange themselves into geometric shapes—crystals. Geller remembers the wonder she felt seeing snowflakes under her father's microscope. "He showed me the relation between geometry and nature, and I have always been fascinated with it," said Geller. "So it's no accident that I would do projects like these maps." Geller went on to become the second woman to ever earn a PhD in physics at Princeton University.

Geller believes that maps are changing our picture of the universe. "Mapping galaxies gives the night sky something that simply looking at it won't provide: the third dimension," she wrote. Her team has now measured the distances and positions of more than 10,000 galaxies. That sounds like a lot, but it's actually only about 0.001 percent of what's out there. "About the fraction of Earth

that is covered by the state of Rhode Island," wrote Geller.

Thanks to Geller's team, we now know that the universe has an overall pattern to its structure. It's made up of many squashed-together, galaxy-covered bubbles of dark voids. Matter in the universe isn't evenly distributed at all. It's instead concentrated on the edges of vast regions of nothing. Why is the universe spongy? Has it always been full of holes? No one knows—yet.

Luckily, the answers are out there because what happened long ago is still observable. "The universe is a time machine," said Geller. "When we look out in space, we look back in time." Seeing something a few billion light-years away is also seeing the universe as it was a few billion years ago. The history of the universe is still out there. All we have to do is look for it.

LOOKING FAR AND DEEP

Looking far enough out into the universe to see back in time takes telescope power. By the early 1980s, telescopes were powerful enough to see galaxy clusters some 5 billion light-years away. The light coming from the

clusters left the galaxies 5 billion years ago. Their ancient light was hot and blue, like star-forming galaxies. Nearer galaxies are cooler, redder, and more static or unchanging. Looking back in time was revealing a different cosmos.

Our universe did not simply explode into its current form. Its galaxies have evolved and changed over time. A new telescope made this crystal clear in 1995. It was something completely different, a telescope that was also a satellite: the *Hubble* Space Telescope.

The crew of space shuttle *Discovery* launched the *Hubble* Space Telescope (HST) from its cargo bay on April 25, 1990. Astronomers around the world have been lining up to use it ever since.

As an orbiting spacecraft, the HST is above our atmosphere and its blurring effects. The telescope satellite has a clear view to the stars. A researcher can wait many years for his or her chance to see a particular planet, comet, galaxy, or star with the HST. So spending 10 whole December days in 1995 pointing the telescope toward the same starless spot of sky wasn't popular

Soap Up Some Galaxy Clusters

When Margaret Geller and John Huchra mapped their first slice of the sky, they discovered that galaxies clustered on the outside of bubble-like voids. Create your own 3-D map of bubbles to better visualize the universe's structure.

YOU'LL NEED

➡ 3 flexible drinking straws

➡ Masking or painter's tape

➡ Cup

➡ Liquid dish soap or bubble solution

➡ Water

➡ Thin straw, such as a coffee stirrer or cocktail straw

➡ Piece of clear, hard plastic or glass

1. Bend the tops of the three drinking straws, then make a triangle out of them by pinching one end of each one and slipping it inside the end of another.

2. Set the straw triangle on a dry countertop or waterproof tabletop. Use the masking tape to anchor and seal around the outside of the triangle. Does your slice look a bit like the galaxy survey slice on page 96?

3. In a cup, dilute some liquid dish soap by mixing in water—about 1 tablespoon for ¼ cup of water. Pour and spread a very thin layer of the mixture (or you can use an undiluted bubble solution) inside your triangle.

4. Make some bubbles! Set one end of the coffee stirrer straw into the soapy layer and blow to create a bubble. Carefully pull out the straw without popping the bubble. Move the straw to a new area inside the slice and repeat. Keep this up until you've created a half-dozen or so bubbles of different shapes and sizes. (Hints: Hold the straw as close to perpendicular to the countertop as you can to create the best bubbles. You may need to add extra soap, or use a deeper layer of the soap mixture on the countertop.)

5. Rub some of the soap water on one side of a piece of clear plastic. (Repeat step 4 if your bubbles have disappeared.) Without popping the bubbles, gently set the piece of clear plastic or glass soapy-side down on top of the bubbles so they flatten out, as in a cross-section. Look familiar? You've created a map similar to the Stick Man image. The outer, shiny soapy film is like the galaxies that surround the empty bubble-shaped voids in the universe.

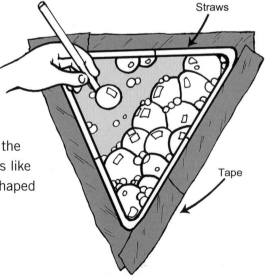

Straws

Tape

Where Are We Exactly?

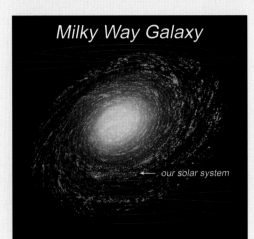

Milky Way Galaxy

← our solar system

Our sun is one of 100 thousand million stars in the Milky Way galaxy. Galaxies themselves belong to groups. The Milky Way is one of 20 or so galaxies in a group that is 5 million light-years in diameter, called the Local Group.

The Andromeda galaxy is the biggest member of the Local Group with 400 trillion stars, four times as many as the Milky Way. The Local Group is on the edge of a cloud of galaxies that are part of the Virgo Supercluster. More than 1,000 galaxies belong to the Virgo Supercluster, yet it is only a tiny speck in the universe.

Local Galactic Group

Milky Way

Andromeda

Virgo Supercluster

our local group

Observable Universe

← Virgo Supercluster

Andrew Z. Colvin

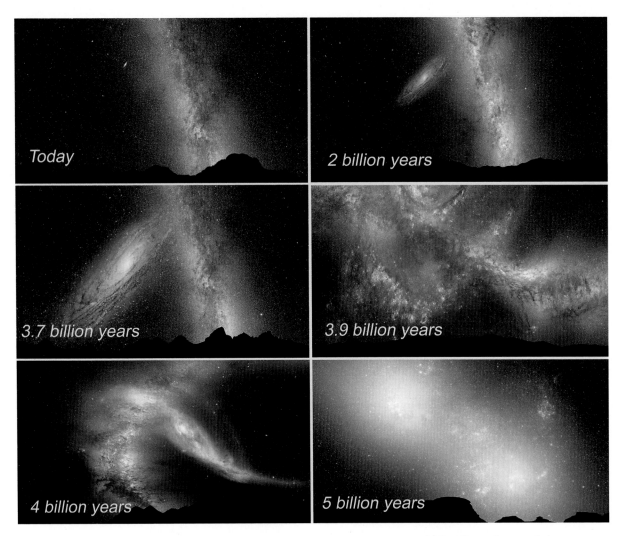

Today

2 billion years

3.7 billion years

3.9 billion years

4 billion years

5 billion years

This series of photo illustrations shows the predicted collision between our Milky Way galaxy and the neighboring Andromeda galaxy, as it will likely happen over the next several billion years.

NASA, ESA, Z. Levay and R. van der Marel (STScI), T. Hallas, and A. Mellinger

with everyone. But the picture of the teeny bit of night sky not far from the Big Dipper's handle was extraordinary. The Hubble Deep Field image was our deepest, farthest, longest-ago look at the universe yet. It showed a colorful cosmos full of spiral, elliptical, and irregular galaxies that moved and changed shape.

The Deep Field image is like a scenic snapshot that happens to capture a train wreck happening in the background. Galaxies are seen smashing into each other, colliding and merging, growing and disappearing. It turns out that the universe is a demolition derby of galaxies. Gravity pulls things together, clumping dust into planets, condensing gas into stars, and shoving galaxies into each other.

Galaxy collision is just another part of how the universe evolves. Smashed-up galaxies make new stars and elements, recycling the old into something new. Our own galaxy will slam into our nearest galactic neighbor in several billion years. "Andromeda is on a collision course with the Milky Way," said Margaret Geller.

PLANETS BEYOND OUR SUN

Is there anybody out there? People have been asking this since the earliest stargazers looked up at the night sky. Whether or not we are alone in the universe is a question that Geoff Marcy has pondered from childhood. "When you look up into the night sky, you see thousands of twinkling lights," said Marcy. "Those are stars, like our sun." Geoff Marcy is a planet hunter. He's an astronomer who looks for alien worlds beyond our solar system, called extrasolar planets or **exoplanets**. These are **alien planets** that orbit other suns. Marcy was part of one of the teams that discovered exoplanets in 1995.

The Swiss team of Michel Mayor and Didier Queloz came in first. They began planet hunting in the spring of 1994 at the Geneva Observatory. Stars beyond our solar system are far away. Any alien planet that might be orbiting one of these distant suns would look tiny and dim through a telescope as compared to its host star. It would be like trying to see a firefly next to a bonfire— impossible. No one was trying to directly

An improved and updated camera on the *Hubble* Space Telescope gave us an even farther and longer-ago view in 2004. The Ultra Deep Field captured some 10,000 galaxies—this from a patch of sky small enough to fit inside a big moon crater.

NASA, ESA, and S. Beckwith (STScI) and the HUDF Team

Our Galactic Group in 3-D

activity

Our galaxy, the Milky Way, belongs to a group of galaxies within a 5 million-light-years wide neighborhood called the Local Group. Galaxies of all three major shapes—spiral, elliptical, and irregular—can be found in the Local Group as well as a variety of types within the spiral and elliptical shapes (see diagram on page 67). A fun way to appreciate the variety of galaxies in the Local Group is by mapping them in 3-D.

YOU'LL NEED

➡ Graph paper

➡ Pencil

➡ Square piece of polystyrene or florist foam, at least 1 foot square and 1 inch thick (glue two chunks together if necessary)

➡ Glue

➡ Galaxy-maker materials in three colors (index cards, cotton balls, glitter, beads, clay, markers, etc.)

➡ Ruler with centimeters

➡ Long wooden skewers

➡ Scissors

➡ Black poster board (optional)

➡ Black paint (optional)

1. Make a 20 by 20 grid on graph paper. Make the grid as large as possible but so it still fits on your piece of foam.

2. Label the boxes along the bottom *x*-axis of the grid with the letters A through T, from left to right. Label the boxes on the left-side *y*-axis of the grid 1 to 20, from bottom to top. Box 1A will be in the lower left-hand corner and 20T in the top right. Repeat labels on the top *x*-axis and right-hand *y*-axis. This will make locations easier to find in all regions, as with an atlas grid.

3. Glue the graph paper grid onto the square piece of polystyrene or florist foam. Study the chart on page 105. It features 15 of the brightest galaxies in the Local Group. They are divided into the three basic galaxy shapes and their more specific types, too. The grid position on the chart is the location where the skewer for that galaxy will go on the foam grid. The height of the skewer gives the galaxy's third dimension.

4. Make galaxy markers! These will be glued on top of each skewer and represent a galaxy on the chart. You can use something as simple as three colors of

beads or stickers—red for spiral, green for elliptical, and blue for irregular galaxy types. Or you can cut out spiral shapes, elliptical shapes, and irregular shapes from colored index cards, or create them from cotton balls, clay, or whatever else is around and color with markers and glitter. (Images of each of the 15 galaxies are easy to find in books and on websites, if you want to customize each one.)

5. Measure the skewers to each galaxy's height, using the chart. Starting at the skewer's pointy end, use a centimeter ruler and a pencil to measure and mark, then cut with scissors. If your skewers aren't long enough, glue two together.

6. Assemble and place each galaxy. For example, find the 31-cm skewer, glue the Andromeda cutout (or the spiral color marker) to it, and push it into the foam at box 9E. Repeat the process for each of the galaxies.

Optional: Turn your Local Group into a diorama by surrounding two or three sides with some black poster board and painting the skewers and grid black.

Galaxy Type	Galaxy Name	Grid Position	Height (in cm)
Spiral			
Sb	Andromeda, M31	9E	31
Sb/c	Milky Way	15D	16
Sc	Triangulum, M33	6F	15
Elliptical			
E0	Leo II	19H	9
E0	Draco	16J	21
E2	Fornax	12I	8
E2	Le Gentil, M32	9L	31
E3	Leo 1	19G	1.5
E3	Caldwell 18/NGC185	11O	29
E4	Ursa Minor	16K	18
E5	Caldwell 17/NGC147	11P	33
E6	M110/NGC205	8M	33
Irregular			
	Large Magellanic Cloud	14Q	12
	Small Magellanic Cloud	14R	13.5
	Caldwell 51/IC1613	12S	13

Great Space Telescopes

The goal of NASA's Great Observatories Program was to study the universe with space-based telescopes that could see across the electromagnetic spectrum. The *Hubble* Space Telescope (HST) can see in visible as well as in ultraviolet and near-infrared light. Its instruments and optics have been upgraded by astronauts a number of times since its 1990 launch.

The second Great Observatory space telescope was the *Compton* Gamma-Ray Observatory (CGRO). From 1991 until 2000 it observed high-energy gamma rays from some of the most violent happenings in the universe.

The *Chandra* X-Ray Observatory went to work in 1999 studying X-rays from black holes, quasars, supernovas, and other objects billions of light-years away.

The *Spitzer* Space Telescope was the only of the four Great Observatories to launch atop a rocket. The other three went into orbit from a space shuttle. In 2003 the *Spitzer* began detecting infrared energy, or heat, coming from the centers of galaxies, newly forming planetary systems, and regions where stars are forming. The Earth's atmosphere blocks most of this kind of infrared radiation, so it can't be viewed from telescopes on the ground.

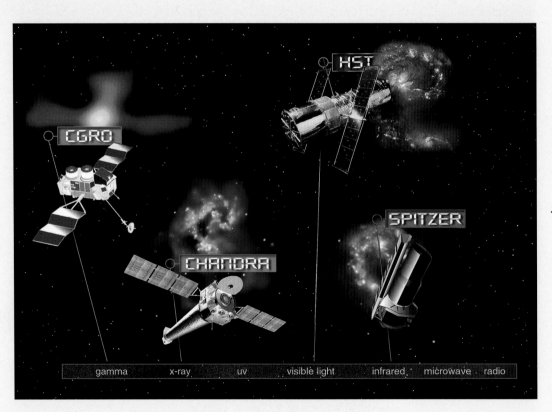

The Antennae galaxies look very different across the electromagnetic spectrum. The same object was observed by all four of the Great Observatory telescopes.

NASA/CXC/M.Weiss

observe an exoplanet orbiting an alien sun, like we've seen Saturn or Neptune.

So how did Mayor and Queloz discover the first exoplanet after only 18 months of looking? They scanned the skies for stars that showed signs of being tugged on by something the size of a planet. Like an invisible leash, gravity from an orbiting planet pulls on its sun through the bend in space-time. You might not be able to see the planet, but you can see evidence of the star being yanked around. A tugged-on star wobbles a bit and its light quivers. "So if you just watch the star, you see it move to and fro," explained Marcy.

Quivering starlight from a wobbling sun is exactly what the Swiss team saw in the star 51 Pegasi. It is 45 light-years away in the constellation Pegasus and is roughly the size of our own Sun. The cause of its wobble is a very hot **gas giant** planet about half the size of Jupiter, named 51 Peg B and informally called Bellerophon. Discovering the first exoplanet forever changed humanity, said Marcy. "We now know, as a species, that there are other worlds out there."

Bellerophon orbits a star similar to our Sun, but it doesn't behave like any of our

eight planets. The giant gaseous exoplanet circles 51 Pegasi once every 100 hours! That means a year on Bellerophon is only 4 days long. The discovery puzzled and stunned astronomers and planet hunters like Geoff Marcy. No one expected to find a gas giant planet so close to its star. Bellerophon is closer to its sun than Mercury is to ours.

Our solar system's gas giant planets, such as Jupiter or Uranus, are far from the Sun, cool, and take *decades* to complete their orbits. The Swiss discovery made astronomers realize that planets elsewhere could be very different. Most hadn't thought that a gas giant planet could exist so close to a star. The discovery made Geoff Marcy realize that he might have missed something.

Marcy had been looking for exoplanets for eight years before Bellerophon was dis-

Left: Astronomer Geoff Marcy and his team have discovered more than 250 exoplanets. *NASA*

Right: This illustration shows what a hot gas giant exoplanet such as 51 Peg B might look like. *ESA–C.Carreau*

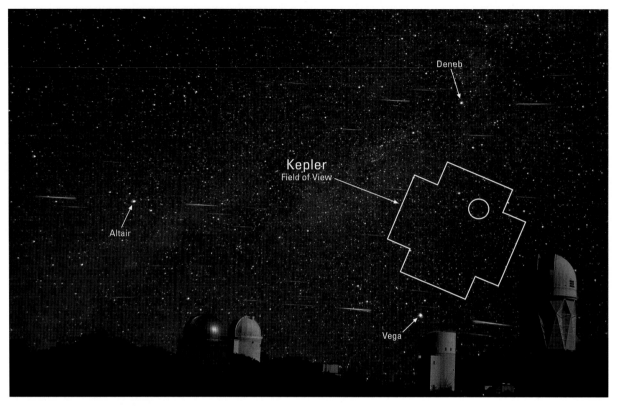

Left: Engineers ready the *Kepler* Space Telescope for its 2009 launch. *NASA/JPL-Caltech/Ball*

Right: The outlined section of the sky surveyed by *Kepler* as seen over Kitt Peak National Observatory. *J. Glaspey, P. Marenfeld & NOAO/AURA/NSF*

covered. After it was found, he went back and looked through all the information his team had gathered. Were there some wobbling stars that might have planets in fast orbits near their stars that they'd overlooked? There were two: a gas giant seven times as big as Jupiter around the star 70 Virginis and another world closely orbiting the star 47 Ursae Majoris.

Soon, exoplanet discoveries came pouring in. Of the first 100 found, 70 were identified by Geoff Marcy.

TAKING THE SEARCH TO SPACE

Tracking down exoplanets by their wobbling stars has limits. Only big planets shake their stars. You won't see any wobble if the planet is the size of our home planet. And rocky, small planets are exactly what astronomers seek. "We want to find Earths," explained Marcy. He meant planets like Earth in size and in their distance from a Sun-like star. Worlds that are not too hot or too cold for water to exist. Habitable planets where alien life might live. "We want to know whether we're alone," Marcy said. "And *Kepler* is the first mission that can find true twins of our earth."

Kepler is a space telescope that went into orbit in 2009. Its mission is to look for habitable Earthlike planets around other stars. The powerful telescope is above the blur of the atmosphere and has a clear view of 150,000 stars in the Milky Way. It isn't looking for wobbles. Instead, it is searching for smaller planets by detecting a kind of eclipse called a **star transit**. When a planet passes (or transits) in front of a star, it blocks out the patch of light created by its shadow. The planet's sun dims by a tiny amount during a planet's star transit. This dimming is what *Kepler* detects.

Within the first three years of its mission, *Kepler* found thousands of planets beyond our solar system, including the first rocky exoplanet, the first small planet in the habitable zone of a star, as well as both Earth- and Mars-sized planets. "We should know, within our lifetimes, whether there are other Earths and whether some, or most, of them are habitable, like our own Earth," said Marcy. "What a lucky time to be alive."

A RUNAWAY UNIVERSE

Saul Perlmutter started measuring galactic speeds in the mid-1990s. He is an astrophysicist and supernova expert. Supernovae are dying stars that shine super-brightly as they explode. Their brightness makes them useful markers of distant galaxies. "We know

by just the brightness of the supernova how far away it is and hence, how far back in time that particular explosion occurred," explains Perlmutter. By plotting where distant galaxies' supernovae are located and when each blew up, Perlmutter's team was able to measure how fast those galaxies moved.

The project was similar to how Edwin Hubble figured out that the universe is expanding in 1929. Hubble observed that

Astrophysicist Saul Perlmutter was one of three scientists awarded the Nobel Prize in 2011 for discovering that the expansion of the universe is accelerating.

Lawrence Berkeley National Laboratory

Track Down Exoplanets

activity

The telescope onboard Kepler searches for exoplanets by looking for the dimming of starlight caused when a planet passing in front of it casts its shadow on the star. Model the effects of star transits on a sun of alien planets in this activity.

YOU'LL NEED

⇒ Table tennis ball

⇒ Sharpened pencil

⇒ Small flashlight or reading light

⇒ Tape

⇒ Fishing line

⇒ Round beads of different sizes

⇒ Scissors

⇒ Dark-colored paper

1. Carefully poke a hole in a table tennis ball with a pencil tip. Fit the light bulb from a small flashlight into the ball, or secure the ball onto the light. (You may need to remove the light bulb's cover, widen the hole in the ball, or affix it with some tape to make it work. Important: the light must still turn on and off.) This represents the star.

2. String a single bead onto a cut length of fishing line and knot it. Do this with a few other beads. These represent alien exoplanets of various sizes.

3. Find or create a dark backdrop for the star. A dark corner can work, as can simply folding a sheet of dark paper in half to make a corner. Turn the star's light on and the room lights off. Dangle different planets in front of the star, circling them around it as if in orbit. Notice how the light changes on both sides of the dark corner. How does the size of the planet affect how much the star's light dims?

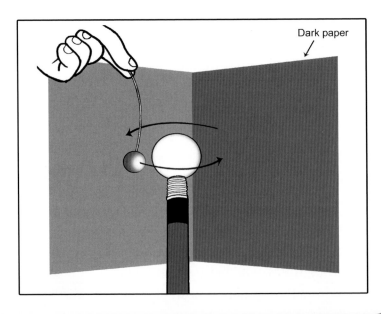

Light bulb cover from small flashlight

Hole

Dark paper

galaxies are moving away from us. But Perlmutter's supernovae team measured how fast the universe is stretching out by comparing supernovae in near and far galaxies. They expected to find that the farthest galaxies would move the fastest. Why? Because what is farther out in the universe is older than what is close. Distant galaxies are part of the newborn universe of long ago, so these ancients should be speeding away more quickly from the Big Bang. Gravity slows things down over time. Therefore, the younger, closer galaxies should be moving more slowly since the universe is now stretching out less quickly than it did right after the Big Bang. Or so they thought.

When Perlmutter's supernovae team compared the brightness of distant and nearby supernovae in 1998, they got a big surprise. The faraway supernovae were fainter and farther away than expected—they were moving away too fast. The expansion wasn't losing speed. "When we started getting results that showed . . . in fact it wasn't slowing at all—it was speeding up—it was a pretty big shock," said Perlmutter.

How could the expansion of the universe be accelerating? It goes against common sense. You toss an apple into the air and gravity eventually pulls it down. "What we were seeing was a little bit like throwing the apple up in the air and seeing it blast off into space," said Perlmutter.

Other teams of scientists were finding the very same results. The expansion of the universe is definitely speeding up. The discovery has big consequences. First, it means the universe is older than we thought. It also means that the universe is ripping apart in all directions and that its galaxies are becoming farther apart, diluting the cosmos until everything will eventually spread out into infinity. Even more troubling is the fact that an accelerating universe goes against the laws of gravity.

EINSTEIN'S ERROR OR DARK ENERGY?

Gravity supposedly rules the universe. It compresses gas into stars, clumps dust into planets, and swings planets around suns. According to Einstein, gravity does all this by bending and warping space-time. The mass of and distance between objects deter-

This diagram shows how the expansion of the universe has sped up since the Big Bang. The shallower the curve, the more the universe is expanding and the faster that objects within it separate. Astronomers theorize that dark energy is pushing galaxies apart.

Ann Feild (STScI)

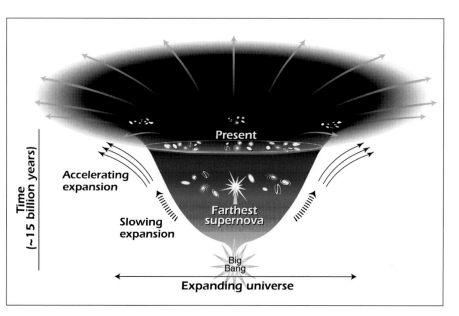

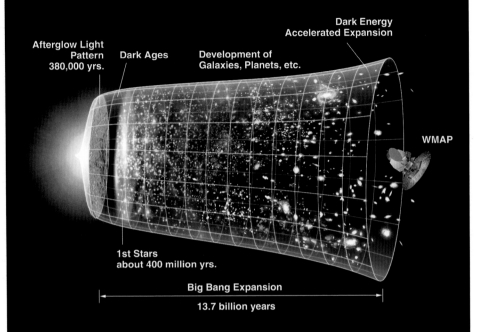

Afterglow Light
Pattern
380,000 yrs.

Dark Ages

Development of
Galaxies, Planets, etc.

Dark Energy
Accelerated Expansion

WMAP

1st Stars
about 400 million yrs.

Big Bang Expansion

13.7 billion years

The afterglow radiation seen by WMAP was emitted about 380,000 years after the Big Bang. This illustration shows the map WMAP created.

NASA / WMAP Science Team

mine their gravitational pull on each other. What is working against gravity and moving galaxies apart faster and faster? Why is the universe's expansion accelerating?

One possibility is that Einstein's theory of gravity is wrong. Isaac Newton's theory of gravity explains most of what we experience every day—falling fruit, an orbiting moon, flying jets, etc. General relativity wasn't necessary until the vast distances between stars and the speed of light were added to the human experience. "It's also possible that Einstein's theory of general relativity . . . may

need . . . a little bit of a tweak when you use it to describe things on the huge scale of the universe," says Perlmutter. But he isn't ready to throw out Einstein yet.

Perhaps our understanding of space itself is missing something. Maybe empty space is actually filled with a mysterious, invisible, so-called **dark energy**. And perhaps dark energy is simply a normal property of space, maybe even a kind of invisible energy field like electricity or magnetism.

Albert Einstein figured out that space wasn't nothing, incorporating it into the

bending fabric of space-time. An early version of his gravity theory included a cosmological constant, an unknown force that works against gravity, keeping the universe from collapsing. Whatever it is, could dark energy be causing our runaway universe?

If dark energy is the culprit, it likely exists in all empty spaces—the space between stars, the space between you and this book, the space between molecules, the space between protons and electrons. "Any space at all in the universe would have some of this energy that's basically making space want to reproduce itself faster and faster," explains Perlmutter. Dark energy could be adding more space to existing space, stretching out space and accelerating the universe's expansion in the process.

MAPPING THE DARKNESS

Dark energy isn't a minor detail. It's the bulk of the universe. Nearly three-quarters of the universe is dark energy. That's about the percentage of Earth's surface that is covered in water. Astronomers know this thanks to a small spacecraft called WMAP. The *Wilkinson* microwave anisotropy probe

(WMAP) launched in 2001, a few years after the discovery of dark energy. Its mission is to measure cosmic microwave background (CMB) radiation, the heat afterglow of the Big Bang.

WMAP's sensitive instruments measure and map the tiny temperature variations in CMB across the sky. WMAP has given astronomers a detailed picture of the newly born early universe before galaxies existed. The spacecraft also spent more than seven years measuring what the universe is made of.

It turns out, there isn't much you'd recognize. Atoms make up only 1/20 of what's in the universe. Everything you can touch, smell, feel, and see makes up 4.6 percent of the universe—every star, planet, person,

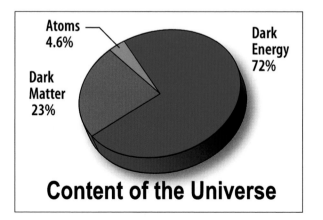

Content of the Universe

speck of dust, molecule of gas, water, comet, tree, and solar system. The rest is invisible.

The other ingredient in the universe besides dark energy, and a sprinkling of atoms, is **dark matter**. Like dark energy, dark matter is invisible and mysterious. Unlike dark energy, dark matter isn't a new scientific mystery. In the 1930s, astronomer Fritz Zwicky was trying to add up the mass of a cluster of galaxies. He had a good estimate of what it should be based on a sum of all the stars' likely masses as calculated from their analyzed starlight. But when he tried to double-check the mass of each galaxy by measuring their speeds of motion, he was way off. Unseen matter in every galaxy seemed to be giving stars an extra weighty pull along their orbit. But that extra mass was missing and immeasurable—dark matter.

Astronomers can observe the effects of dark matter's gravity on surrounding matter.

NASA / WMAP Science Team

While it has gravity and bends space-time, dark matter is not made up of atoms, nor their subatomic parts—protons, neutrons, and electrons.

What is in dark matter? No one knows yet. One idea is WIMPs (weakly interacting massive particles)—unusual, undetectable subatomic particles that might form dark matter. No matter what it is, dark matter is in control. With more mass than normal matter composed of atoms, the gravitational attraction of dark matter rules. It determines what clumps and condenses, crashes and orbits. Dark matter formed the universe we know, and dark energy now fills it. The universe is mostly controlled by and composed of unseen stuff!

After thousands of years of observation and centuries of scientific study, the cosmos has given up very few secrets. The universe remains mostly unknown and overflowing with discoveries yet to even be imagined.

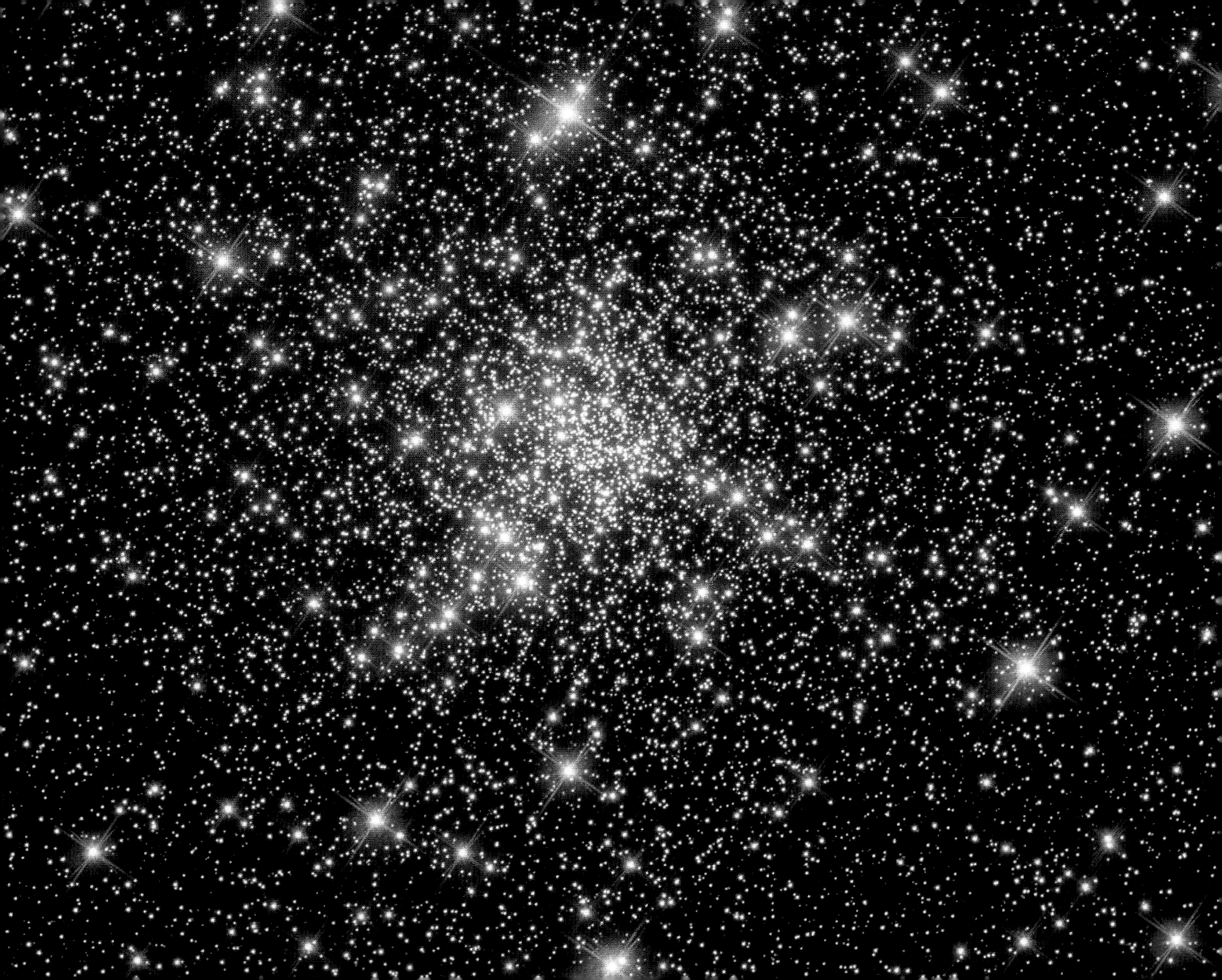

Afterword
What Will We Find Next?

What are astronomers, stargazers, and space scientists on the verge of discovering in the next decades?

Exactly what will be learned about the universe in upcoming years is hard to say, but new findings are guaranteed. Why? Because so many basic questions remain unanswered! Dark energy shapes the universe, yet we don't know what it is—or even how to detect it. Other fundamental ingredients and happenings are just as mysterious, from how supernovas happen to where cosmic rays come from.

The focus of ongoing research in astronomy and astrophysics right now can be summed up into three big, basic questions.

➡ **Cosmic Dawn:** *How did all of this get here?* Studying how the universe came into existence and produced galaxies.

➡ **Universe Physics:** *What makes up the universe and how does it work?* Learning how all kinds of matter,

energy, space, and time behave, interact, and make it all happen.

➡ **New Worlds:** *Are we alone?* Planets and planetary systems around other suns will shed light on how our own solar system's planets came into being. It could also lead us to unimaginable worlds where life may someday be found.

How will these questions be studied and their answers' revealed? Technology has fueled cosmic discoveries for many centuries—from grinding glass for early telescopes to satellites and computers. New radio and optical telescopes, particle colliders, and other technological advancements will further expand scientists' view. There are also a fleet of orbiting observatories, satellites, and space telescopes being readied for launch. *NuSTAR* will study the universe in high energy X-rays; *GEMS* will zoom-in on black holes and neutron stars; the mission of *ST-7/Lisa Pathfinder* is to detect and measure gravitational waves; and dark energy and dark matter is among the

Left: The *James Webb* Space Telescope has a primary mirror made of folding segments.

ESA (C. Carreau)

Right: Engineers prep some of the primary mirror segments of the *James Webb* Space Telescope for testing.

NASA/Chris Gunn

mysteries up for studying by *Astro-H*'s suite of onboard telescopes.

And then there's the *Webb*. The *Webb* is the *James Webb* Space Telescope (JWST). The space telescope is set to launch in 2018 and is the successor to the *Hubble* Space Telescope. Like the *Hubble*, the *Webb* will be a shared tool used by thousands of researchers around the world over its decade-long life. Yet unlike the *Hubble*, the *Webb* will mostly take images in infrared. Remember

that the farther away an object is, the further back in time it is. Seeing in infrared will allow the *Webb* to see some of the first galaxies created, those that are moving away so quickly that the light they emit gets shifted toward the red end of the spectrum.

Collecting enough light to see almost as far back as the Big Bang is tricky. Infrared light is heat, so to be able to detect distant heat the telescope itself needs to be super cold. An onboard cooling unit will help,

as will being far out in space. *Webb* won't orbit Earth; it will instead sit out about 930,000 miles (1.5 million km) from Earth. The *Webb* will also have a giant 21-foot (6.5 meter) **primary mirror** for collecting infrared light. The mirror is seven times the size of *Hubble*'s, so engineers designed it as segments that fold up during launch and then unfold once in space. The *Webb* promises to once again change our view of the universe and our place in it.

Glossary

alien planet a planet orbiting a star other than our sun; an exoplanet

astrolabe an instrument for observing the positions of stars and other space objects

astronomer a scientist who studies stars, planets, and other space objects

astronomy the science of the stars, planets, galaxies, and the universe

astrophysics a kind of astronomy that studies the physical and chemical properties of space objects

atmosphere the layers of gases that surround a star, planet, moon, or other space object

Big Bang theory the scientific theory that the universe began and expanded after a powerful explosion of a small amount of extremely dense matter

binary star two stars that orbit around each other

black hole a void in space left when a large star dies and collapses, creating such strong gravity that anything nearby is sucked into it—including light

Cepheid a variable star with a regular, predictable cycle of brightness

comet a space object made of dust, frozen water, and gases that orbits the Sun

concave hollowed or rounded inward, like the inside of a bowl

constellation a group of stars that are imagined to resemble a named shape

convex curved or rounded outward, like the outside of a ball

Copernican system a solar system in which planets move in circular orbits around the Sun; a heliocentric system

cosmic microwave background (CMB) radiation cooled, faint radiation that fills the universe and is left over from the Big Bang

cosmos the universe

dark energy an unknown force that is likely causing the universe to expand

dark matter an unknown form of matter that is invisible

deferent the orbit around Earth of an epicycle

diameter the length of a straight line passing through the center of a circle or sphere

diffraction grating a prism-like device used to separate wavelengths of light. It is usually made of glass, plastic, or metal, with tiny parallel lines etched into its surface

eclipse the total or partial shadowing of one space object by another

electromagnetic (EM) radiation electromagnetic energy such as gamma rays, X-rays, ultraviolet light, visible light, infrared radiation, microwaves, and radio waves

electromagnetic (EM) spectrum the entire range of electromagnetic radiation types

electromagnetism magnetism produced by an electrical current

elliptical shaped like an elongated, closed curve, or oval-shaped

epicycle a small circle whose center moves around in the circumference of a larger circle

eyepiece lens the lens of a telescope that is nearest the eye of the observer

exoplanet an extrasolar planet, a planet orbiting a star other than our sun

frequency the number of vibrations that a sound wave or light wave makes in one second

galaxy a group of billions of stars that orbit a common center point

gamma ray shortwave electromagnetic radiation of very high frequency

gas giant large gaseous and liquid planets with no land, such as Jupiter

general relativity Einstein's theory that describes gravitation by the curvature of space and time.

geocentric having Earth at the center, as in the Ptolemaic system

gravity the force of attraction between two objects; the shape of space-time

heliocentric having the Sun at the center, as in the Copernican system

Hertzsprung-Russell Diagram (H-R Diagram) a graph that plots star spectral types against magnitude, star temperature, and color versus brightness, or luminosity

Hubble's Law the observation that the redshift in light coming from distant galaxies is proportional to their distances from us

inertia a property of matter by which it remains at rest or in unchanging motion unless acted on by some external force

infrared light invisible electromagnetic radiation that has a long wavelength and that is experienced as heat

light-year a unit of length in astronomy equal to the distance that light travels in one year—about 5.88 trillion miles (9.46 trillion km)

luminosity the amount of light emitted by a star; brightness

main sequence star a star like the Sun

mass the amount of matter in an object

matter any kind of substance that takes up space

microwave electromagnetic radiation, characterized by a long wavelength

Milky Way the galaxy to which the Sun, our solar system, and all the visible stars in the night sky belong

NASA the National Aeronautics and Space Administration; the US space agency

nebula a cloud of gas and dust in space. Some nebulae are located where new stars are being formed, others are what's left of dead or dying stars.

neutron star the dense leftover core of a dead massive star, made mostly of neutrons

nova an explosion from a medium or small star

nuclear fusion the combining of two atomic nuclei to create a nucleus of greater mass

objective lens the lens of a telescope that is nearest the object being observed

optical telescope a telescope through which visible light is observed

orbit a specific path followed by a planet, satellite, or other space object, caused by the gravity of the space object it's traveling around

parallax the angle between two imaginary lines from two different observation points, which can be used to estimate distance

photon a particle of light

physics the science of matter, energy, and interactions between the two

planet a round space object that orbits the Sun and is alone in its orbit

Polaris the North Star

primary mirror the main light-gathering surface of a reflective telescope

prism a clear, solid object with flat faces used to separate white light into rainbow colors

Ptolemaic system Ptolemy's theory that Earth is at the center of the universe; a geocentric system

pulsar a fast-spinning neutron star that is a source of powerful radio waves emitted in short, intense, regularly occurring bursts or pulses

quasar a galaxy-like object that emits powerful ultraviolet light and radio waves

radio astronomy the detection and study of radio waves from space

radio galaxy a galaxy that gives out as much energy in radio waves as it does in light

radio wave the type of electromagnetic radiation that has the lowest frequency and the longest wavelength; it is produced by charged particles moving back and forth

red giant an old, dying star that has swollen larger, so is bright but cool

redshift a shift in the light of stars and galaxies toward the longest wavelength (red) end of the spectrum due to the expansion of the universe

reflecting telescope a telescope that focuses incoming light on a mirror

refracting telescope a telescope that focuses incoming light through a lens

relativity Einstein's theory that describes the physical laws that determine time, space, mass, motion, and gravity as relative to the observer

retrograde moving in a backward direction

rotation the spin of a space object

satellite an object that orbits around a larger space object; for example, a moon or an artificial satellite, such as a weather satellite or the *Hubble Space Telescope*

solar wind the continuous stream of charged particles released from the Sun outward into space

space-time four-dimensional space that includes time along with width, height, and length

spectral type a star's color classification that tells you its temperature; O, B, A, F, G, K, or M

spectroscope an instrument that separates light and other electromagnetic radiation into their various wavelengths

spectroscopy the study of spectra to determine the chemical composition and physical properties of substances

spectrum a band of colors that forms when light passes through a prism

star a space object, made of hot gases, that radiates energy

star transit a planet or other space object's passage in front of a star

starscape the background pattern of stars seen in the night sky

sunspot a magnetic storm on the Sun's surface that shows up as a dark area

supercluster a group of galaxy clusters

supernova a massive exploding star

telescope an instrument for making distant objects appear nearer and larger

ultraviolet light invisible electromagnetic radiation that has a very short wavelength

universe all of space, in which everything in existence is contained

variable star a star that changes in brightness over time

visible light electromagnetic radiation that human eyes can see

wavelength the distance between two adjacent peaks of a wave of light, sound, or other energy

weight the force exerted on mass by gravity

white dwarf a tiny, dim, hot, dense, leftover core of a dead star

X-ray penetrating electromagnetic radiation with an extremely short wavelength

zenith the point in the sky directly overhead

Resources

ASTRONOMY WEBSITES TO EXPLORE

Amazing Space
http://amazing-space.stsci.edu/
This is the education gateway of the Space Telescope Science Institute (STSci), home to the *Hubble* Space Telescope and all its amazing imagery. From here you can view the *Hubble* gallery, do online explorations about astronomy, and even enroll in the "Hubble Deep Field Academy."

Chandra X-ray Center
http://chandra.harvard.edu/edu/
The website of the orbiting space telescope *Chandra* X-Ray Observatory is packed full of astonishing images from the telescope, as well as Space Scoop for Kids, podcasts, interactive games, printable posters and calendars, and classroom activities.

Imagine the Universe
http://imagine.gsfc.nasa.gov
Older kids and teens will enjoy this site, which was created by the High-Energy Astrophysics Science Archive Center. It's full of the latest news about space travel and the universe, detailed resources, activities, and Ask an Astrophysicist.

NASA Educational Resources
www.nasa.gov (click: For Educators)
NASA has a huge variety of resources for teachers and other educators, from activities and information to media of all kinds.

NASA Quest
http://quest.nasa.gov
This site contains web-based, interactive explorations designed to engage students in authentic scientific and engineering processes related to NASA projects.

Space Place
http://spaceplace.nasa.gov
NASA's fun website for kids features all kinds of information, games, projects, and fun activities.

Starchild
http://starchild.gsfc.nasa.gov
This comprehensive site for elementary and some middle school students has information on the solar system, universe, and space science at two reading levels.

Windows to the Universe
www.windows2universe.org
A comprehensive site about the universe and space science, written at three reading levels from which visitors may choose. The site includes many resources for teachers, too.

SKY WATCHING AND STAR CHART SITES

These sites will help you find what you're looking for in the night sky—from moon phases and constellations to meteor showers and the current positions of the planets.

> www.space.com/skywatching/
> http://stardate.org/nightsky/
> www.skyandtelescope.com/observing/ataglance
> http://amazing-space.stsci.edu/tonights_sky/
> http://heavens-above.com
> www.fourmilab.ch/yoursky/

BOOKS FOR FURTHER READING

Bartusiak, Marcia. *Archives of the Universe: A Treasury of Astronomy's Historic Works of Discovery*. New York: Pantheon Books, 2004.

Bartusiak, Marcia. *The Day We Found the Universe*. New York: Pantheon Books, 2009.

Couper, Heather, and Nigel Henbest. *The History of Astronomy*. Richmond Hill, Ont.: Firefly Books, 2009.

Glass, Ian S. *Revolutionaries of the Cosmos*. Oxford: Oxford University Press, 2006.

Herrmann, Dieter B. *The History of Astronomy from Herschel to Hertzsprung*. Cambridge, MA: Cambridge University Press, 1984.

Murdin, Paul. *Secrets of the Universe: How We Discovered the Cosmos*. Chicago, IL: University of Chicago Press, 2009.

Panek, Richard. *Seeing and Believing: How the Telescope Opened Our Eyes and Minds to the Heavens*. New York: Viking, 1998.

Panek, Richard. *The 4 Percent Universe: Dark Matter, Dark Energy, and the Race to Discover the Rest of Reality*. Boston, MA: Houghton Mifflin Harcourt, 2011.

Pendergrast, Mark. *Mirror Mirror: A History of the Human Love Affair with Reflection*. New York: Basic Books, 2004.

Index

Page numbers in *italics* indicate pictures.